Think Like a Trader, Invest Like a Pro

Think Like a Trader, Invest Like a Pro

CHRISTINA RAY

McGraw-Hill
New York Chicago San Francisco Lisbon London Madrid
Mexico City Milan Montreal New Delhi San Juan
Seoul Singapore Sydney Toronto

Library of Congress Cataloging-in-Publication Data

Ray, Christina I.
   Think like a trader, invest like a pro / by Christina Ray.
     p. cm.
   ISBN 0-07-136467-6
   1. Investments. 2. Securities. 3. Investment analysis. I. Title

HG4521.R33 2001
332.6—dc21

                                                                          00-048201

McGraw-Hill

A Division of The **McGraw·Hill** Companies

Copyright ©2001 by McGraw-Hill. All rights reserved. Printed in the United States of America. Except as permitted under the United States Copyright Act of 1976, no part of this publication may be reproduced or distributed in any form or by any means, or stored in a data base or retrieval system, without the prior written permission of the publisher.

1 2 3 4 5 6 7 8 9 0   DOC/DOC   0 7 6 5 4 3 2 1

ISBN 0-07-136467-6

The sponsoring editor for this book was Catherine Dassopoulos, the editing supervisor was Ruth W. Mannino, and the production supervisor was Elizabeth Strange. It was set in Century Schoolbook by Judy Brown.

Printed and bound by R. R. Donnelley & Sons Company.

This publication is designed to provide accurate and authoritative information in regard to the subject matter covered. It is sold with the understanding that neither the author nor the publisher is engaged in rendering legal, accounting, or other professional service. If legal advice or other expert assistance is required, the services of a competent professional person should be sought.

          —*From a Declaration of Principles jointly adopted*
                by a Committee of the American Bar
            Association and a Committee of Publishers.

McGraw-Hill books are available at special quantity discounts to use as premiums and sales promotions, or for use in corporate training programs. For more information, please write to the Director of Special Sales, Professional Publishing, McGraw-Hill, Two Penn Plaza, New York, NY 10121-2298. Or contact your local bookstore.

 This book is printed on recycled, acid-free paper containing a minimum of 50% recycled de-inked fiber.

CONTENTS IN BRIEF

Preface   xvii

PART ONE
TECHNICAL ANALYSIS

1. The Tools and Techniques of Professional Traders   3
2. Traders and Trading   7
3. Current Market Prices   11
4. Market Color and Flow   43
5. Price History, Charting, and Pattern Recognition   81
6. Analytic Indicators and Models   95

PART TWO
FUNDAMENTAL ANALYSIS

7. Economic News and Numbers   107
8. Corporate Actions, News, and Rumors   121

PART THREE
TRADE SELECTION

9. Fundamental Screening, Back Testing, and Securities Selection   149
10. Technical Screening, Back Testing, and Model Creation   161
11. Expert Opinions and Recommendations   177

PART FOUR
RISK, REWARD, AND PERFORMANCE MEASUREMENT

12. Risk Measurement   193
13. Portfolio Optimization   209

INDEX   227

CONTENTS

Preface xvii

PART ONE
TECHNICAL ANALYSIS

Chapter 1
The Tools and Techniques of Professional Traders 3

Chapter 2
Traders and Trading 7
    The Institutions 8
    The Goal 9
  A TYPICAL COMPOSITE SCREEN 10
    Figure 2–1 Multi-Window Display from WindowOnWallStreet 10

Chapter 3
Current Market Prices 11
    Price Quality 11
    The Role of Auctioneers 12
    The Role of Agents 12
    The Role of Dealers 13
    The Computer as Auctioneer 15
    Trader Jargon: Reading Traders' Minds 16
    Parsing Trader Jargon 17
  REAL-TIME STOCK QUOTES 22
    Figure 3–1 Real-Time Stock Quote for Intel from MSN 22
    Figure 3–2 Intraday Price Chart for Intel from MSN 23
  A REAL-TIME LOOK AT ELECTRONIC EXCHANGE BOOKS 24
    Figure 3–3 A Real-Time Book for Yahoo! from Island 24

A REAL-TIME ELECTRONIC EXCHANGE BOOK IN CHART FORM 26

Figure 3–4   2D Chart of the Cisco Book from 3DStockCharts   26

COMPARING FLOW IN REAL-TIME ELECTRONIC EXCHANGE BOOKS 28

Figure 3–5   Dueling Books Display for Yahoo! and eBay from Quotezart   28

FUTURES MARKET QUOTES ON THE CME 30

Figure 3–6   Quotes for the S&P and Eurodollar Contracts from DBC   30

FUTURES MARKET QUOTES ON THE CBOT 32

Figure 3–7   Quotes for the Dow Jones and 30-Year Bond Contracts from CBOT   32

QUOTES FOR OPTIONS ON FUTURES ON THE CBOT 34

Figure 3–8   Quotes on Treasury Bond Options from TradeSignals   34

CUSTOMIZING A COMMODITY WATCH SCREEN 36

Figure 3–9   Customized Commodity Watch Screen from TradeSignals   36

QUOTES ON LISTED STOCK OPTIONS 38

Figure 3–10   Quotes for Options on Sprint Corp. from Quote   38

Chapter 4

Market Color and Flow 43

MONITORING FLOW ON THE NYSE AND THE NASDAQ 45

Figure 4–1   LiveChart Price History for a Nasdaq-Listed Security from Quote   45

Figure 4–2   LiveChart Price History for a NYSE-Listed Security from Quote   46

FLOW OVER TIME 48

Figure 4–3   Three-Dimensional Chart of Cisco from 3DStockCharts   48

GRAPHIC STATISTICS FOR FLOW OVER TIME 50

Figure 4–4   Nasdaq Order Book and Chart for Exodus as of July 21, 2000, from FalconEye   50

CONTENTS ix

Figure 4–5   Market Sleuth for Morgan Stanley Dean Witter
              as of July 21, 2000, from FalconEye   52
AUTOMATING LIMIT ORDER CALCULATION   53
Figure 4–6   Order Optimizer for Microsoft from FalconEye   53
**DERIVING FUTURE EXPECTATIONS
FOR INTEREST RATES   55**
Figure 4–7   U.S. Treasury Yield Curve: One-Day Change
              from Bloomberg   55
**IDENTIFYING ORDER IMBALANCES
ON A REAL-TIME BASIS   59**
Figure 4–8   Musical Quotes for Nasdaq Stocks on Island
              from Quotezart   59
Figure 4–9   Buy/Sell Ratio for Nasdaq Stocks on Island
              from Quotezart   60
**MONITORING INSTITUTIONAL
INTEREST MESSAGES   62**
Figure 4–10   Institutional Activity for Nokia from Thomson   62
Figure 4–11   Institutional Activity for Philip Morris
              from Thomson   65
COMPARING INDEX SHARES   66
Figure 4–12   Price and Volume Data for Index Shares
              from Nasdaq   66
MONITORING COMMODITY PRICES   68
Figure 4–13   Commodity Movers from Bloomberg   68
ANTICIPATING THE TRADING DAY   70
Figure 4–14   Most Active Stocks: Premarket and After Hours
              from Nasdaq   70
**IDENTIFYING CHART PATTERNS
AND TRIGGER LEVELS   72**
Figure 4–15   Multiday 15-Minute Bar Chart for Broadcom
              from BigCharts   72
ANTICIPATING THE NEXT DAY   74
Figure 4–16   Top Stock Options Ranked by Volume from Quote   74
SPOTTING CHANGES IN VOLATILITY   76
Figure 4–17   Implied Volatility Chart for Infinity Broadcasting
              from Optionetics   77

Figure 4–18 Stock Options Ranked by Breakouts in Implied Volatility from Optionetics   78
LISTENING TO LIVE COLOR   80

Chapter 5

Price History, Charting, and Pattern Recognition   81
The Inefficient Market Hypothesis   82
Trader Psychology and Trigger Events   83
UNDERSTANDING THE FOUNDATIONS OF CHARTING   84
Figure 5–1 Relative Strength with Volume at a Price Chart from Bridge   84
CONSTRUCTING TREND LINES   87
Figure 5–2 Interactive Java Chart with Trend Lines from CNET   87
SELECTING THE APPROPRIATE CHARTING PERIOD   89
Figure 5–3 Year-to-Date Price History for Salton, Inc. from MSN   89
Figure 5–4 Three-Month Price History for Salton, Inc. from MSN   90
IDENTIFYING KEY PRICES   91
Figure 5–5 Intraday Bond Futures Price Chart from CBOT   91

Chapter 6

Analytic Indicators and Models   95
IDENTIFYING A CHANGE IN TREND   97
Figure 6–1 Salton Chart with Moving Averages from MSN   97
FINDING EXPERT TECHNICAL AIDS   99
Figure 6–2 Price and RSI Chart of Microsoft from TradeStation   99
Figure 6–3 Drop-Down Menu of Analysis Techniques from TradeStation   100
Figure 6–4 Automated Expert Analytic Commentary from TradeStation   101
IDENTIFYING TRENDS IN VOLATILITY   102
Figure 6–5 Chart of Implied Volatility and Technical Indicators for VIX from BigCharts   102
Figure 6–6 BigCharts Glossary of Analytic Terms   103

CONTENTS   xi

PART TWO
FUNDAMENTAL ANALYSIS

Chapter 7
Economic News and Numbers   107

TRACKING THE ECONOMY   109
Figure 7-1   Economic Calendar from Yahoo   109
Figure 7-2   Economic Calendar Terms from Yahoo   110

STUDYING THE DETAIL   112
Figure 7-3   Employment Situation News Release from BLS   112

WATCHING THE FED CALENDAR   114
Figure 7-4   Federal Reserve Calendar from FederalReserve   114

WATCHING THE FED   116
Figure 7-5   Fed Watch from Bloomberg   116
Figure 7-6   FOMC Announcement Dates from Bloomberg   117

GETTING REAL-TIME ECONOMIC NEWS   119
Figure 7-7   Market Monitor from Bloomberg   119

Chapter 8
Corporate Actions, News, and Rumors   121

WATCHING THE EARNINGS CALENDAR   123
Figure 8-1   Earnings Calendar from MSN   123
Figure 8-2   Earnings Surprises for Limited, Inc. from MSN   124
Figure 8-3   Earnings Estimates for Limited, Inc. from MSN   125
Figure 8-4   Price History with Corporate Actions for Limited, Inc. from MSN   126

REAL-TIME ALERTS OF NEWS AND RUMORS   127
Figure 8-5   News Alerts for All Securities from TheFlyOnTheWall   127
Figure 8-6   Site Cross Reference for Exodus Communications from TheFlyOnTheWall   128
Figure 8-7   Daily Price Chart for Exodus Communications from TheFlyOnTheWall   130

RESEARCHING COMPANY FILINGS   131
    Figure 8–8   Recent Filings for Sprint, Inc. from Edgar-Online   131
    Figure 8–9   Price Chart of WorldCom, Inc. versus Sprint Corp. from MSN   135

EVALUATING IPOS   136
    Figure 8–10   IPO.com Index for July 19, 2000, from IPO   136
    Figure 8–11   Offering Information for Support.com on July 19, 2000, from IPO   137

LISTENING TO INSIDER TALK ON IPOS   139
    Figure 8–12   IPO "Deals in Demand" Report for July 17, 2000, from TheFlyOnTheWall   139
    Figure 8–13   Detail about Blue Martini Software from TheFlyOnTheWall   140
    Figure 8–14   News and Events for Support, Inc. on July 19, 2000, from TheFlyOnTheWall   141
    Figure 8–15   Chart of Support, Inc. on July 19, 2000, from TheFlyOnTheWall   142

KEEPING UP WITH THE NEWS   143
    Figure 8–16   New Ideas in Technology from Validea   143
    Figure 8–17   Buzz Report for Solectron Corp. from Validea   144

LINKS TO NEWS SOURCES   145
    Figure 8–18   News and Analyst Links for Exodus Communications from JustQuotes   145

PART THREE

TRADE SELECTION

Chapter 9

Fundamental Screening, Back Testing, and Securities Selection   149

SCREENING FOR TRADE IDEAS   151
    Figure 9–1   Stock Finder Custom Screen from MSN   151
    Figure 9–2   Chart of Celera Genomics with Technical Indicators from MSN   153

BACK-TESTING FUNDAMENTAL CRITERIA   154
    Figure 9–3   Stock Finder Search for Low P/E from MSN   154
    Figure 9–4   Stock Finder Search for High P/E from MSN   155

USING PREDEFINED SEARCHES BASED ON FUNDAMENTAL DATA 156

    Figure 9–5   Predefined Fundamental Searches from WallStreetCity 156

    Figure 9–6   Projected Growth Stocks with Reverse Potential from WallStreetCity 157

VIEWING GRAPHIC REPRESENTATIONS OF VALUE 158

    Figure 9–7   Predefined Fundamental Searches as of July 21, 2000, from WallStreetCity 158

    Figure 9–8   M*Stock Grades for Polycom from WallStreetCity 160

Chapter 10

Technical Screening, Back Testing, and Model Creation 161

USING BACK-TESTED SEARCHES BASED ON TECHNICAL DATA 163

    Figure 10–1   ProSearch Technical Search and Back Test from WallStreetCity 163

    Figure 10–2   Chart of Moving Average Breakout Criteria for Dimeco Inc. on July 20, 2000, from WallStreetCity 165

SEARCHES BASED ON OPTION PARAMETERS 166

    Figure 10–3   ProSearch Option Model Definition from WallStreetCity 166

    Figure 10–4   ProSearch Option Search Results from WallStreetCity 169

    Figure 10–5   Details about Option and Underlying Security from WallStreetCity 170

    Figure 10–6   Research Wizard Alerts for First Security Corp. as of July 22, 2000, from MSN 171

VISUAL SCREENING FOR REAL-TIME TRADE IDEAS 173

    Figure 10–7   Tracker as of July 21, 2000, from FalconEye 173

    Figure 10–8   Tracker Interpretations from FalconEye 174

Chapter 11

Expert Opinions and Recommendations 177

REVIEWING ANALYSTS' OPINIONS 179

Figure 11–1 Summary of Brokerage Recommendations on July 20, 2000, for Exodus Communications from MultexInvestor 179

Figure 11–2 Research Reports Available for Exodus on July 20, 2000, from MultexInvestor 181

QUALIFYING ANALYSTS' OPINIONS 182

Figure 11–3 Snapshot of Opinions about Exodus Communications from BulldogResearch 182

Figure 11–4 Detail of Earnings Estimates for Exodus Communications as of July 18, 2000, from BulldogResearch 183

Figure 11–5 Industry Stock Picking Awards for Computer Software from BulldogResearch 185

Figure 11–6 Chart of Computer Software as of July 18, 2000, from BigCharts 186

GETTING THE FULL STORY 187

Figure 11–7 Listing of Audio Events for July 19, 2000, from StreetEvents 187

GETTING EXPERT TECHNICAL COMMENTARY 189

Figure 11–8 Expert Comment on AM S&P Futures Activity on July 20, 2000, from TradingMarkets 189

Figure 11–9 Daily Tick Chart for Sep 2000 S&P 500 Futures from eSignal 190

PART FOUR

RISK, REWARD, AND PERFORMANCE MEASUREMENT

Chapter 12

Risk Measurement 193

The Risk Measurement Process 194
The Tools 195
Risk as a Forecast 195

TRACKING PORTFOLIO PERFORMANCE 196

Figure 12–1 Return Analysis for Custom Portfolio from MSN 196

Figure 12-2   Chart of Homestake Mining versus Morgan Stanley Dean Witter as of July 21, 2000, from MSN   197
Figure 12-3   Price Performance Chart for Custom Portfolio from MSN   198

MEASURING PORTFOLIO RISK   200

Figure 12-4   Portfolio Risk Report for Custom Portfolio from RiskGrades   200

MEASURING RISK FOR OPTIONS ON FUTURES   202

Figure 12-5   Analysis of Options on Bond Futures from Optionomics   202

MEASURING RISK FOR EQUITY OPTIONS   204

Figure 12-6   Risk Report for Options on Microsoft from Optionomics   204

ESTIMATING THE RISK OF A TECHNICAL TRADING STRATEGY   206

Figure 12-7   MACD Strategy Simulation for Microsoft from TradeStation   207
Figure 12-8   MACD Strategy Performance Report for Microsoft from TradeStation   208

Chapter 13

Portfolio Optimization   209

Portfolio Design, Restructuring, and Optimization   210
Wave Systems: A Classic Liquidity Squeeze   211
The Warnings   213

MEASURING PORTFOLIO RISK   214

Figure 13-1   Custom Portfolio as of July 25, 2000, from FinPortfolio   214
Figure 13-2   Chart of Southwest Airlines and Exxon Mobile from MSN   215
Figure 13-3   Risk-Adjusted Return Report from FinPortfolio   216
Figure 13-4   Value at Risk Report from FinPortfolio   217
Figure 13-5   Market Exposure Report from FinPortfolio   218
Figure 13-6   Asset Allocation Report from FinPortfolio   219

PERFORMING AN ASSET SEARCH   220

Figure 13-7   Quantitative Criteria for Portfolio Asset Selection of July 28, 2000, from FinPortfolio   220

Figure 13–8   Search Result for Asset Selection of July 28, 2000,
                from FinPortfolio   221
RECOGNIZING DANGER SIGNS   222
Figure 13–9   Price Chart for Wave Systems
                from Omega Research   222
Figure 13–10   Implied Volatility Chart for Wave Systems
                from Omega Research   223
Figure 13–11   Chart of Risk Grade for Wave Systems
                from RiskGrades   224
Figure 13–12   Value at Risk Analysis for Wave Systems
                as of July 28, 2000, from FinPortfolio   225

INDEX   227

PREFACE

The Internet is an amazing resource. As a former trader who's used to having my firm supply me with the best information that money can buy, I'm astonished by how close the Internet comes to providing me with the same tools I've become accustomed to, and at little or no cost.

Availability of these tools has narrowed the information gap between the professional and the amateur. At the same time, it has increased the level of confusion on the part of the individual investor. As recent studies show, an overwhelming amount of data can reduce clarity instead of increasing it. And, there exist so many alternative versions of the same information that it's difficult for the individual investor to identify which ones are of Wall Street quality.

In selecting sites for inclusion in this book, I've favored those that present information in the style and format I'm accustomed to as a trader. Traders are fussy about presentation, and there are usually good, practical reasons for display in one format rather than another.

At the same time, I've found innovative sites that present data in ways that didn't exist till recently. To be sure, professional traders are using these sites as well.

I have excluded from consideration sites that require the individual to open a brokerage account. However, many of these brokerage sites have excellent tools their customers should take advantage of.

Many of the sites I've included provide both delayed data (often for free) and real-time data for a fee. This expense is generally a function of the data, because most of the exchanges sell that data on a monthly basis. Fortunately, they charge individual investors less than institutions. Depending on trading style, the delayed data may be good enough for many investors. Most premium analytic sites also allow free trial subscriptions of up to 30 days.

Wall Street traders use the term *seat rent* to describe the expense to the firm of supporting a single trader. At some firms seat rent is over $5 million per year, and the firm considers that it has not broken even until the trader has generated profits of this amount. I hope that this book serves to minimize the seat rent and increase the profitability of my readers.

Christina Ray

Think Like a Trader, Invest Like a Pro

PART ONE
Technical Analysis

Technology reigns at each trader's desk, and each trader has a choice of myriad sources of information to focus on any given day. A trader may customize the computer's screens to display whatever prices and data the trader considers most critical today. This data may come from public sources, such as Bloomberg or Bridge Data, or proprietary sources, such as systems created by the firm's Research and IT (Information Technology) departments.

Each trader has upward of 100 direct lines to select counterparties and brokers. Those who trade commodities such as S&P or bond futures may also have a dedicated squawk box that provides continuous quotes and commentary from the floors of the CBOT (Chicago Board of Trade) or the CME (Chicago Mercantile Exchange).

Chapters 3 through 6 describe how institutional traders use current market prices and price history to assist them in predicting future market behavior.

CHAPTER 1

The Tools and Techniques of Professional Traders

If there is a single characteristic common to all successful investors, it's their intense awareness that the market is no more than the sum of its participants. The ones who know this best are locals and market makers at the commodity exchanges, who observe market flow and attach a name to each order as it comes into the pit. The ones who know this least are on-line day traders, who observe changes in the market as depersonalized video displays.

Investors who are able to view the market in such human terms have an edge in predicting future market movements. They know that market moves appear random when investors' actions tend to offset each other, but appear systematic when they act in unison.

Institutional investors are expert at anticipating situations in which a large number of investors—or an important minority—are likely to act in unison. They know that certain stimuli are capable of triggering a collective response. Typical trigger events for a stock, for instance, are the release of an economic statistic, an earnings report, a substantial change in price, or even just the passage of time. Likewise, when well-regarded portfolio managers go on CNBC to tout positions they already own, they're actually manufacturing a trigger event.

The power of such trigger events stems from their ability to arouse human emotions. And all investors, whether individual or institutional, are motivated by two dominant emotions: fear and greed. When faced with the imminent prospect of missing enormous gains or incurring catastrophic losses, they operate with a greater sense of urgency, chasing the market both up and down and creating recognizable patterns.

Some economists would disagree with this interpretation. They contend that the markets are *efficient*, that is, that at any point in time, the price of a security reflects all information currently known about it. Forecasting future market prices with only public information is therefore impossible, and portfolio managers who consistently beat market averages are merely a statistical aberration.

Any professional trader knows otherwise. Professional traders know that people are not computers, instantly deriving a value for each security as they digest each new piece of information. Professional or amateur, they take time to act, they are influenced by what went before, they get excited, and they make mistakes.

Therefore, the most valuable skill professional traders possess is their ability to identify trigger events that might cause certain classes of investors to act in concert. And because the root source of these investors' behavior is grounded in human nature, their reactions form patterns that repeat time and time again. So, an investor who is in tune with the euphoria or angst of the marketplace can often predict the market's reaction to an important trigger event—both the instantaneous reaction and how it plays out over time.

Dr. Antonio Damasio has studied the biology of emotions as it impacts the process of good decision making.[1] He refutes the notion that the best decisions are the most dispassionate ones. Instead, he contends that our ability to reason is as likely to be harmed by a lack of emotion as by an excess of emotion.

> Let's say that you are trying to make a complicated decision. If you try to do a cost-benefit analysis, it may take you forever to decide whether to do A or B. However, if you have previously been in similar situations, and if you have been either rewarded or punished by the choices you made in those situations, then emotional memory may help you with your current choice. It may come in the form of a gut feeling or, more subtly, in the form a nonconscious bias that leads you in a certain direction.

Dr. Damasio goes on to point out that depending on emotional memory doesn't always work. "If you have not had the right experiences, or if you have not classified your experiences in a good way, your emotional memory could be leading you in the wrong direction."

Institutional traders—if they're good—gradually develop the ability to recognize patterns in market behavior at both a conscious and unconscious level. The information and tools available to traders in a state-of-the-art trading room provide them with both the raw and derived data that eventually become their library of relevant experience.

Skilled traders recognize the market advantage that internalizing pattern recognition gives them. They are not embarrassed to justify some trading decisions based on no more than subconscious "gut feel," a term that wrongly implies gambling rather than forecasting. Although such decisions may at times be flawed, they are fast—an advantage often more important than any other.

---

[1] *New York Times,* May 7, 2000.

The following chapters are designed to assist the individual investor in developing similar skills by using resources available over the Internet in the same way a professional might. By having the right experiences, by opening their eyes to patterns everywhere, and by classifying these experiences in terms of investor behavior, they can learn to predict the behavior of others as well as improve their own.

CHAPTER 2

Traders and Trading

The world of institutional traders is an exclusive one. The number of traders who have substantial trading authority is probably only in the low thousands worldwide. Those in the same specialty (for example, all bond option traders) often know each other, and are able to make fairly precise guesses about the motives and style of one of their competitors or clients when they identify one of their trades.

These guesses are, for the most part, based on the institution for which the trader works and the trader's function at that institution, rather than on any individual idiosyncrasies. The type of institution for which the traders work determines the types of positions they may take, their ability to take risk, and the horizons they consider most relevant to their trading.

Nevertheless, all traders have one thing in common: they are paid annual bonuses based on performance. Traders' bonuses are generally the bulk of their annual compensation, and can be several times their salary. Similarly, fund managers report performance at least quarterly, if not monthly. And showing regular performance is critical in gathering new assets to manage. Thus, the horizon for both traders and the institutions for which they work is seldom greater than a few months, and is often much less.

So the tools and techniques that professionals use are intended to assist them in meeting their companies' goals as well as their own.

THE INSTITUTIONS

Trading institutions generally fall into one of two categories: *asset managers* or *dealers*. Asset managers, such as mutual fund sponsors Fidelity or Putnam, invest money that belongs to individuals or other institutions, while dealers, such as Morgan Stanley Dean Witter, take positions with the corporation's own assets. These two functions are distinct from that of a *broker,* who may only act as an agent for the customer. Nevertheless, some firms are broker/dealers and perform both functions.

An asset manager generally makes money in two ways: by earning a good return on the assets it manages, and by increasing its asset base. Generally, mutual funds do not employ leverage, although *hedge funds*—funds with a limited number of relatively wealthy and sophisticated investors—may.

Of course, the two ways are correlated: outstanding performance can generate performance-based fees on AUM (Assets under Management). And regular ROI (Return on Investment) quarter after quarter is the pattern that is most likely to attract new money.

Conversely, a dealer is primarily interested in maximizing its profit within risk limits. It may employ massive amounts of leverage in some areas. For example, the Treasury desk—the area that trades Treasury bills, bonds, and notes—may employ leverage of 100:1 in some strategies. Therefore, ROI is not as relevant for such an institution as is return relative to risk taken. Of course, now that most of the large dealers are public institutions, some of the gunslinger reputations of the 1980s have been tempered by the need to keep share price up. This is accomplished by showing the same pattern of regular performance to which mutual funds aspire.

THE GOAL

Still, the function of every professional trader is to optimize the risk/return profile: that is, maximize return while constraining the size of losses. And every tool provided in the trading room is designed to assist the trader in this goal. The serious individual investor is a trading desk of one and functions as his or her own risk manager. The individual investor should attempt to replicate the tools, behavior, and discipline of the trading room as much as possible.

A TYPICAL COMPOSITE SCREEN

Source: WindowOnWallStreet.com

Price: Free and Premium

FIGURE 2-1
Multi-Window Display from WindowOnWallStreet

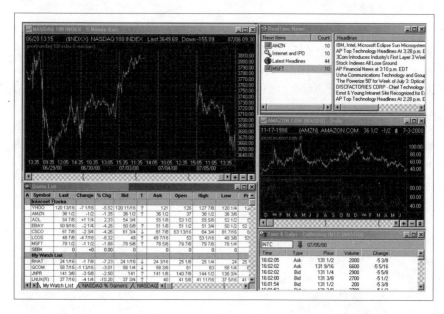

WindowOnWallStreet.com offers the user the ability to customize a professional-style screen composed of multiple windows. In the sample shown, news, prices, Time and Sales reports, and charts all update on a real-time basis.

CHAPTER 3

Current Market Prices

Every tool provided to the professional trader is designed to give the trader an edge over counterparties. And the most important tool available at the trader's desk is continuous access to live market prices for every security or market of interest to the individual trader. The ability to monitor this information is provided to aid the trader in making short-term forecasts, as well as executing transactions in the best possible manner.

PRICE QUALITY

Every professional trader knows the source and the data-collection method of each price quote viewed. This knowledge assists the trader in determining the level of accuracy and the timeliness of the quote, which in turn determines the execution risk the trader might take in placing either a market or limit order.

Quotes supplied over the Internet generally come from one of three sources:

- Exchange floors
- OTC sources
- ECNs (Electronic Communications Networks)

The quality of the quotes depends on the collection mechanism. Some require human intervention, and others are automated. Humans directly responsible for prices generally act as *auctioneers, brokers,* or *dealers.*

THE ROLE OF AUCTIONEERS

An *auctioneer* manages order flow, matching buyers and sellers in the most efficient manner possible, without regard for the identity of the participants. An example of an auctioneer is a specialist on the floor of floor-based exchanges such as the NYSE or Amex. To assist in keeping market flow orderly, one of the specialist's responsibilities is to disseminate price quotes back to the public. The quality of these quotes depends on the specialist; the indications may be precise to the last 100 shares, or they may be reasonable indications of price and size. For example, the auctioneer may show size on the offer of 10,000 shares when total size at that offer may actually be between 10,000 and 15,000 shares.

THE ROLE OF AGENTS

An *agent* can act only on behalf of others. The agent has no trading discretion, only the responsibility to attempt to execute orders from traders. A good broker may improve on the price limit of the order, but is not allowed to take trading discretion. For example, the broker may not hold onto an executable sell order in anticipation that the market will rally.

CHAPTER 3 Current Market Prices

An example of floor brokers are those on the floor-based stock exchanges as well as the commodity exchanges. Brokers charge a commission for their services.

In the case of the floor-based stock exchanges, a floor broker is not required to give orders to the specialist for the security for execution. However, the floor broker must report the transactions to the specialist to allow public price dissemination.

In the case of the commodity exchanges, such as the CBOT and the CME, all trades are executed via "open outcry" in the trading pit. This system facilitates maximum price transparency. The exchanges have price reporters who observe the market action and type in market prices for dissemination.

But professional traders don't rely on these quotes. Instead, they stay on the phone (or listen over a squawk box) to a broker stationed at a booth just outside the pit. Like the price reporters, this broker watches the action in the pit, deciphering much of the raucous flow by use of hand signals. The broker transmits estimates of bid, offer, and size to the customer, ready to flash an order back into the pit if the customer so desires.

Outside of normal exchange trading hours, many of the financial contracts trade electronically: for example, on the CME's Globex system, and on the CBOT's Project A system.

THE ROLE OF DEALERS

Dealers have the discretion to take risk positions on behalf of themselves and their firms as principals to the trade. This right generally comes at the expense of obligations to the marketplace. Dealers provide liquidity to the markets, and take market risk in exchange for an expectation of profit.

Once again, the specialist on the floor of the floor-based exchanges is an example of a dealer, as is a market maker in U.S. Treasury bonds at a firm such as Goldman Sachs or Salomon

Brothers Smith Barney. Dealers do not charge a commission, but profit from advantageous transactions, buying lower and selling higher than the middle of the market. Broker/dealers in the equity markets can act only as brokers or dealers, and must reveal to the customer in which capacity they acted.

On the floor-based stock exchanges, the specialist is required to act as a dealer where necessary to keep market activity orderly and to prevent order imbalances. A specialist whose order book contains a preponderance of sellers, for example, must be willing to bid for the security regardless of the individual's opinion of the price action. Similarly, if the bid/offer spread is very wide, the specialists are expected to narrow it with their own bids and/or offers.

At the Treasury dealer, the U.S. Treasury requires that its *primary dealers* (firms allowed to participate directly in auctions of Treasury securities) make markets to their customers in any Treasury security. Each Treasury desk has traders assigned to a particular part of the yield curve. For example, the *five-year trader* might make markets in each note of maturity greater than two years and less than or equal to five years. If an institutional investor (via an institutional salesperson employed by the dealer) asks for a bid on a $100 million face amount of five-year notes, the market maker must provide the investor with a price to which the market maker will stand up.

This market maker has an expectation of profit (because the market maker is buying on the bid side), but no guarantee of it. The price of the bid depends on the market maker's estimate of the ability to lay the position off within the next few seconds or minutes. For example, if the investor asked for a bid on $500 million notes rather than $100 million, the five-year trader's bid would have been a few 32ds lower.

To lay off a position quickly, the trader relies on one of several interdealer brokers who accept bids and offers from primary

CHAPTER 3 Current Market Prices

dealers or institutional customers and display them on a private network. Quotes for Treasury securities are generally indications derived from an amalgam of the best bids and offers from each broker, and cannot therefore be acted upon.

THE COMPUTER AS AUCTIONEER

The Nasdaq and the ECNs are markets in which computers replace humans in the role of auctioneer and disseminator of price information.

Nasdaq

The Nasdaq is an interdealer market comprising more than 600 securities dealers who act as market makers in the more than 15,000 different securities. The Nasdaq has no trading floor, and securities are not auctioned. Instead, market makers post their best bids and offers for public dissemination. If they fail to do so, they may lose market privileges.

Nasdaq Level II quotes show all bids and offers with size in real time. However, some transactions occur directly between market makers, and may be reported out of sequence. They are so noted in a Time and Sales report, but may create price confusion for the unwary.

ECNs

The ECNs (electronic communications networks) such as Instinet, Island, and Archipelago, automate the function of auctioneer. There are no locals, specialists, or market makers to provide liquidity and buffer large moves. On the other hand, they have total price transparency; traders can view not only the best bids and offers, but all the bids and offers behind them. ECNs may also submit their best bids and offers to the Nasdaq.

Because ECNs are relatively new, they generally have the deepest books and therefore the most reliable indications in newer stocks, such as technology and Internet stocks. They have longer trading hours than the NYSE and Amex, allowing traders to gauge the impact on price of early morning or late afternoon news or earnings reports.

TRADER JARGON: READING TRADERS' MINDS

When asked the current market price of Cisco, an individual investor might respond, "61 1/2"—the price at which Cisco last traded. A professional trader would instead respond, "I'll quote it 61 1/4 at 61 1/2, 5000 by 20,000"—that is, there are 5000 shares bid for at a price of 61 1/4, and 20,000 offered for sale at 61 1/2.

The trader might even add, "But I don't think the offer is for real."

This quoting protocol is common to all traders, irrespective of marketplace. A stock trader, a bond trader, a commodity trader, or a foreign exchange trader would all use nearly identical language. Trader jargon has evolved this way for reasons that have far more to do with utility than custom.

The language of any population reveals what it considers important. The Eskimo language Yupik, which is spoken by about 13,000 people in southwestern Alaska, has more than 15 words for snow. The reasons for distinguishing *muruaneq,* or "soft, deep snow," from *navcaq,* or "snow cornice, about to collapse," are obvious.

Likewise, professional traders are members of their own global population, and its members are also intensely interested in avoiding collapse. Trader language regarding price is the

Rosetta stone of trader-speak, because when seconds count, every syllable is guaranteed to contain critical information.

PARSING TRADER JARGON

Parsing the price quote above will show how traders humanize market prices. In fact, in trader jargon, "offer" can refer to both the price at which someone is willing to sell a security and the person who has made that offer.

First, note that the trader qualified the statement by starting with, "I'll quote it . . ." This choice of words makes clear to the inquirer that the trader is only relaying a snapshot of current market conditions, and is not taking market risk by indicating any willingness to buy or sell the security at the prices indicated. The source of this information might be screen displays of Nasdaq data feeds if the trader is an equity trader at Morgan Stanley, hands in the air if the person is a bond futures trader on the floor of the CBOT, or an educated guess if the individual is an OTC currency trader at Chase.

Next, note that the professional always views price as a region rather than a point: a nebula rather than a star. The bid and offer indicate the range of prices within which the next transaction is likely to occur. And the bid/offer spread indicates the true cost of a transaction, in Cisco, in this case, under current market conditions.

In our example, a round trip in and out of Cisco of 5000 shares or less using a market order will cost 1/4 point (buy at 61 1/2, sell at 61 1/4 = 1/4 loss), not including commissions. For a market maker, this is far too large an expense. And for a fund manager, all those fractions can add up to the difference between mediocre and superior performance over the course of a year.

Further, note that the professional considers *size* (that is, the total quantity bid for and offered at the best bid and offer prices) to be information as critical as the bid and offer prices themselves. Size indicates Cisco's *liquidity*, or the ability to execute large orders in that security without substantially moving market prices.

Although the size on the bid and offer is the total of all bids and offers at that price, the quantity may give the trader a clue about the nature of the counterparties. To the professional, the relatively large size on the offer may indicate that the seller is an institutional rather than individual investor. For example, institutions often trade in 5000-share increments, and quantities that are multiples of this often indicate a single institutional buyer or seller. Further, the professional will realize that the 20,000 shares on the offer may just be part of a 100,000-share order. The seller may be unwilling to show the entire size in one piece for fear of spooking the market lower and accomplishing nothing.

Together, price and size indicate where the next trade might be executed. If a trader submits a *market order* (an order to buy or sell immediately at the best available price), a seller of 5000 shares or less can expect to sell Cisco at 61 1/4, and a buyer of 20,000 shares or less can expect to pay 61 1/2 for Cisco. If the trader attempts to sell more than 5000 shares or buy more than 20,000 shares at the market, the sale may well be filled below 61 1/4, and the purchase filled above 61 1/2.

However, professionals don't usually use market orders when executing a trade. They prefer to take execution risk, because their trading skills usually allow them to trade inside the bid/offer range, that is, buy below the offer price or sell above the bid price. Some, like market makers who may be in a position for only seconds, must attempt to squeeze every penny out of each trade because they work for just a tiny fraction of a point. For example, Treasury bond market makers generally work for only 1/64th of 1 percent.

CHAPTER 3 Current Market Prices

Professional traders frequently use *limit orders* (that is, orders to buy or sell at a specific price) instead of market orders when attempting to execute a transaction. By placing a limit order wisely, a trader expects to improve the price at which the trader enters a new position or exits from an old one. However, use of limit orders exposes the trader to execution risk. A trader who misjudges the tone of the market may have to chase the market to get the trade done at all, often at a level significantly worse than originally anticipated.

Finally, the trader's doubts about the reliability of the offer reveal that the trader has been watching the price of Cisco intently. The trader is not indicating a lack of trust in the quote, but rather questions the bona-fide desire of the trader on the offer to sell 20,000 shares of Cisco. The trader may have noticed that every time the offer is *lifted* (that is, someone pays the offer price), the size of the offer drops.

To a market maker, this pattern may indicate that a savvy trader elsewhere is trying to give the market a false impression: namely, that there are substantial amounts of Cisco available for sale at 61 1/2, in spite of the fact that this trader doesn't really want to sell at all. In fact, it is quite possible that the trader on the offer is really a buyer, attempting to push the market lower in order to buy Cisco cheap.

The offer is taking a calculated risk. Such manipulation is often an effective strategy; a third participant who hasn't been paying attention may be fooled into hitting the 61 1/4 bid before the offer does, helping to drive the price down.

However, the risk in this strategy is the possibility that the trader is unlucky enough to show the offer when a real buyer of size comes into the market and lifts the trader on 20,000 shares. Now, the offer has to chase the price up to buy back both the inadvertent short position as well as the intended purchase.

Based on what they have observed in the market, professionals make very short-term forecasts to enter and exit trades at the best possible level. Let's assume that a professional trader wants to buy 20,000 shares of Cisco now. Not including strategies like the one above, the trader has three choices.

1. Simply lifting the offer at 61 1/2. This is quick and easy, but not the optimal price.
2. Joining the bid at 61 1/4. A trader who believes that the offer at 20,000 is for real may expect to get hit on at least 15,000 shares (the original bidder for 5000 shares will get hit, as well). It seems paradoxical, but increasing the size of the bid in this case may actually increase the probability of the market trading down. This is so because the seller may be reluctant to sell only 5000 shares, lose any 61 1/4 bid, and still have 15,000 shares (or more) to go. If the offer can sell a large block at a relatively good price, the trader will risk driving the market a bit lower.
3. Improving on the 61 1/4 bid: bidding 61 3/16, for example. Although the price isn't as good, the trader is now first in line on the bid, and may entice the offer (or another trader) to hit the bid there. There are variations on this strategy: The buyer may submit just part of a 20,000 share order. An offer who is desperate to sell may hit the 61 3/16 bid and show his hand, turning sentiment a bit more negative for the moment and allowing the buyer to pay 61 1/4 or less for the remaining 15,000 shares.

All these favorable outcomes depend on the fact that the offer is from an institution and is real. An offer who is a large retail investor may not even be watching the price in real time, and all our trader's elaborate games would be for naught. Worse, if the seller wasn't really a seller, the trader's buy orders may instead have 62 *handles* (the integer part of the price) rather than 61 handles when the tickets are finally written.

Although some of these alternatives are just not practical for the individual investor, awareness of these strategies can assist in interpreting price action and placing orders. One mark of the amateur trader is placing a buy order on the bid side just to pay less. If the security trades up, the trader may very well be left behind, unfilled. Orders should be placed where the investor expects the security to trade, rather than where the investor hopes it will trade.

REAL-TIME STOCK QUOTES

Source: MSN.com

Price: Free

FIGURE 3-1

Real-Time Stock Quote for Intel from MSN

Real-Time Quote

Time of last trade: 2:51:00 PM Eastern.

Intel Corporation

Last	115 11/16	Bid/Tick	115 5/8 ↓
Change	+11/16	Ask	115 11/16
Volume	15.3 Mil	Bid/Ask Size	9500 X 100
Day's High	116 5/16	Open	114 9/16
Day's Low	112 3/4	Close	115

Real-Time Intraday Chart

Nasdaq National Market

MSN provides a quick source of real-time prices for equities (Figure 3-1), showing the entire *picture* (bid and offer with size on each), as well as the direction of the last tick. From this quote, a trader might surmise that the 9500 shares on the bid indicate that the next trade is likely to be higher. It also tells the trader the last tick was a downtick, and, as such, a bid at 115 5/8 or lower can't be hit by a short-seller.

CHAPTER 3 Current Market Prices

FIGURE 3–2

Intraday Price Chart for Intel from MSN

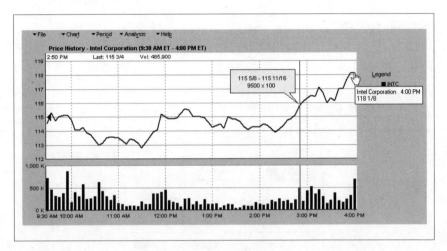

MSN.com's real-time quote feature includes a convenient link to a real-time chart of intraday prices (Figure 3–2). The one-day chart shows that the size on the bid shown in Figure 3–1 may indeed have been a bullish indicator. The price of Intel traded up for the rest of the day, gaining about 2 1/2 points in the hour following that quote.

This chart is interactive: by positioning the cursor at 2:51 P.M. (the time of the real-time quote) a vertical line is drawn down to the volume chart below, showing that substantial volume occurred at that time. And by putting the cursor at the last point on the price line, the box shown at 4:00 P.M. pops up, showing time and price[1] at that point.

---

[1] The annotation regarding bid/offer and size at 2:51 P.M. is the author's.

A REAL-TIME LOOK AT ELECTRONIC EXCHANGE BOOKS

Source: Island.com

Price: Free

FIGURE 3–3

A Real-Time Book for Yahoo! from Island

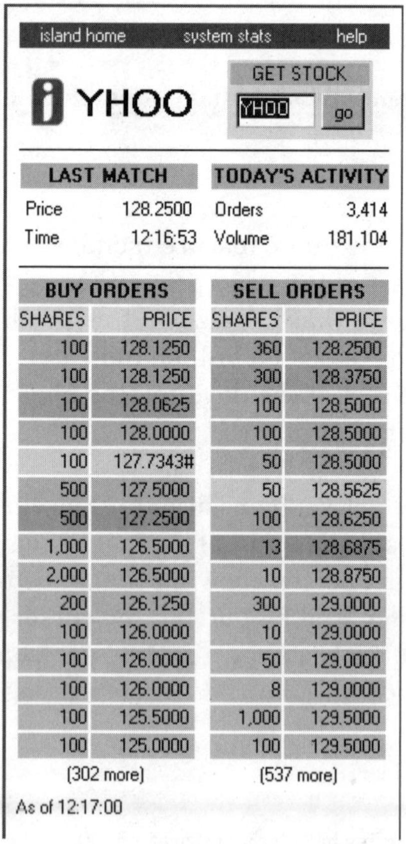
island home system stats help

YHOO

GET STOCK

YHOO go

LAST MATCH		TODAY'S ACTIVITY	
Price	128.2500	Orders	3,414
Time	12:16:53	Volume	181,104

BUY ORDERS		SELL ORDERS	
SHARES	PRICE	SHARES	PRICE
100	128.1250	360	128.2500
100	128.1250	300	128.3750
100	128.0625	100	128.5000
100	128.0000	100	128.5000
100	127.7343#	50	128.5000
500	127.5000	50	128.5625
500	127.2500	100	128.6250
1,000	126.5000	13	128.6875
2,000	126.5000	10	128.8750
200	126.1250	300	129.0000
100	126.0000	10	129.0000
100	126.0000	50	129.0000
100	126.0000	8	129.0000
100	125.5000	1,000	129.5000
100	125.0000	100	129.5000
(302 more)		(537 more)	

As of 12:17:00

CHAPTER 3 Current Market Prices

Island ECN provides the general public with access to its Island "BookViewer": a real-time display of the best limit buy and sell orders in price and time order. Color coding assists traders in identifying blocks of sequential orders at a single price, a feature that is exceedingly useful in a volatile market.

At last count, Island averaged about 12 percent of Nasdaq volume, and often ranks number one in certain stocks such as Amazon, Yahoo!, and eBay. The BookViewer is available during Island's extended trading hours of 7:00 A.M. to 8:00 P.M. It is possible that a trader might see her trade executed on this screen before she receives a report of the trade if her broker routes orders to Island.

A REAL-TIME ELECTRONIC EXCHANGE BOOK IN CHART FORM

Source: 3DStockCharts.com

Price: Free

FIGURE 3-4

2D Chart of the Cisco Book from 3DStockCharts

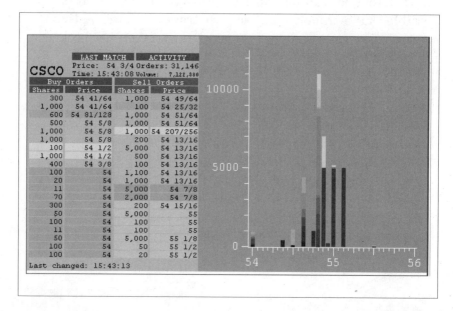

3DStockCharts.com consolidates real-time feeds from two ECNs—Island and Archipelago—and converts the 15 best bids and offers to graphic form. For traders who are visually oriented, 3DStockCharts provides an instant impression of the relative buying and selling pressure. For example, in the snapshot of Figure 3–4, it appears as though it will be difficult for CSCO to trade above 55 or so without fresh buying interest.

3DStockCharts also color codes its displays in order to map the full range of information in the limit order book to graphic form.

COMPARING FLOW IN REAL-TIME ELECTRONIC EXCHANGE BOOKS

Source: Quotezart.com

Price: Free

FIGURE 3–5

Dueling Books Display for Yahoo! and eBay from Quotezart

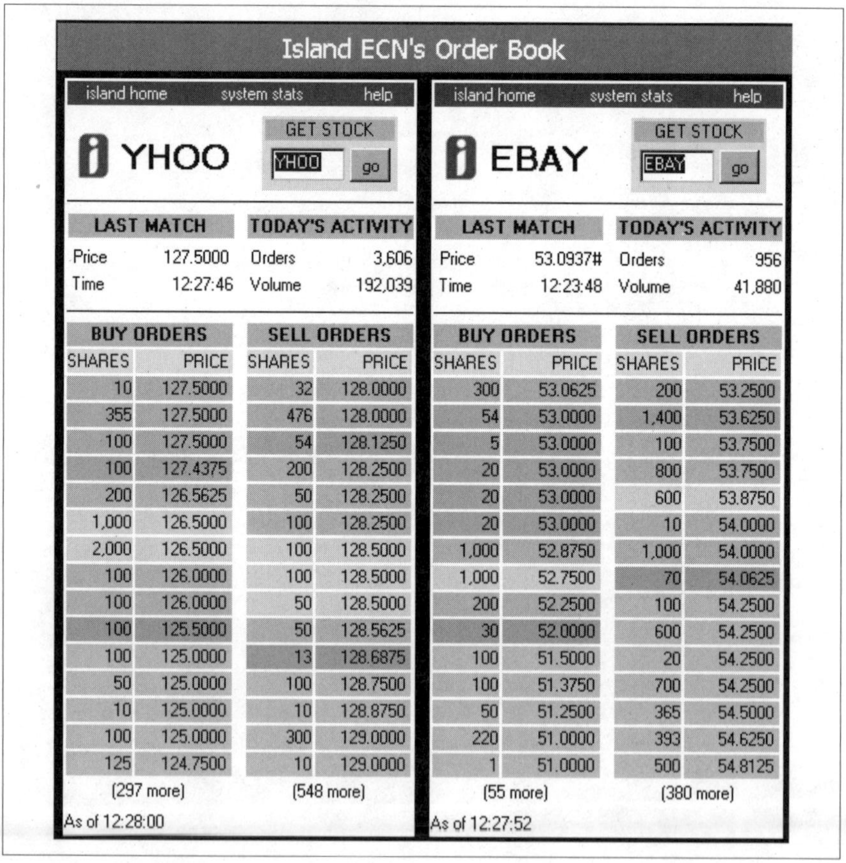

Island ECN's Order Book

island home system stats help

YHOO — GET STOCK: YHOO go

LAST MATCH		TODAY'S ACTIVITY	
Price	127.5000	Orders	3,606
Time	12:27:46	Volume	192,039

BUY ORDERS SHARES	BUY ORDERS PRICE	SELL ORDERS SHARES	SELL ORDERS PRICE
10	127.5000	32	128.0000
355	127.5000	476	128.0000
100	127.5000	54	128.1250
100	127.4375	200	128.2500
200	126.5625	50	128.2500
1,000	126.5000	100	128.2500
2,000	126.5000	100	128.5000
100	126.0000	100	128.5000
100	126.0000	50	128.5000
100	125.5000	50	128.5625
100	125.0000	13	128.6875
50	125.0000	100	128.7500
10	125.0000	10	128.8750
100	125.0000	300	129.0000
125	124.7500	10	129.0000
(297 more)		(548 more)	

As of 12:28:00

island home system stats help

EBAY — GET STOCK: EBAY go

LAST MATCH		TODAY'S ACTIVITY	
Price	53.0937#	Orders	956
Time	12:23:48	Volume	41,880

BUY ORDERS SHARES	BUY ORDERS PRICE	SELL ORDERS SHARES	SELL ORDERS PRICE
300	53.0625	200	53.2500
54	53.0000	1,400	53.6250
5	53.0000	100	53.7500
20	53.0000	800	53.7500
20	53.0000	600	53.8750
20	53.0000	10	54.0000
1,000	52.8750	1,000	54.0000
1,000	52.7500	70	54.0625
200	52.2500	100	54.2500
30	52.0000	600	54.2500
100	51.5000	20	54.2500
100	51.3750	700	54.2500
50	51.2500	365	54.5000
220	51.0000	393	54.6250
1	51.0000	500	54.8125
(55 more)		(380 more)	

As of 12:27:52

CHAPTER 3 Current Market Prices

Quotezart.com provides a "Dueling Books" feature, whereby a trader can view Island ECN's real-time order book for two securities side by side. When those two securities tend to track each other, indications of buying or selling pressure in one of the securities might be a leading indicator of the similar pressure in the other security. Such a short-term forecast could assist a trader in timing a transaction and selecting the best price for his order.

Or, if the two securities were relatively independent of each other but were both market leaders, simultaneous buying or selling pressure might foretell a change in the tone of the general marketplace.

Quotezart.com also converts the information in the order book to the user's choice of musical format, for traders who prefer sound cues to sight cues.

FUTURES MARKET QUOTES ON THE CME

Source: DBC.com

Price: Free and Premium

FIGURE 3-6

Quotes for the S&P and Eurodollar Contracts from DBC

SP U0 USA - Chicago Mercantile Exchange				ED U0 USA - Chicago Mercantile Exchange			
My eSignal • In-depth market analysis • Any time, place or system • Real-time Quote Streamer				*My eSignal* • In-depth market analysis • Any time, place or system • Real-time Quote Streamer			
As of: Jul 06, 2000 @ 7:08 am ET				As of: Jul 05, 2000 @ 2:35 pm ET			
Last Trade: N/A; 10 MIN. DELAY				Last Trade: N/A; 10 MIN. DELAY			
Last	146700	Change	+370	Last	93175	Change	+45
Currency	USD	% Change	+0.25%	Currency	USD	% Change	+0.05%
Open	146350	Tick	-+	Open	93155	Tick	-+-+
Day Low	146300	Day High	146700	Day Low	93155	Day High	93190
Previous	146330	Volume	22,675	Previous	93130	Volume	54,165
Open	146350	Open Interest	365,652	Open	93155	Open Interest	610,410

DBC.com provides quotes on futures contracts, along with the direction of the previous four ticks. These two snapshots show quotes for the Sep 2000 S&P 500 contract and the Sep 2000 eurodollar contract, the most successful financial contracts traded on the CME.

The three-month eurodollar contract is an excellent surrogate for short-term rates, and is the best barometer of changing expectations about possible future rate changes by the Fed. The eurodollar contract is quoted in terms of 100 less the eurodollar interest rate; therefore, the quote of 93.175 (the decimal point always follows the second digit) implies that three-month eurodollar rates starting in September 2000 will be 6.825 percent (100.0 − 93.175 = 6.825). In the futures markets, the front contract (in this case, the September 2000 contract) generally has nearly all of the volume and is the one to watch.

All professional traders—even those who only trade stocks—watch the financial futures contracts as an instantaneous indicator of sentiment about the course of future interest rates. Because the futures trade on a centralized trading floor with an open outcry system, they have more price transparency than any other marketplace, and respond to news nearly instantaneously. Further, the futures markets open earlier than the NYSE and Amex, and some trade electronically all night long. So, their early price action is the most trustworthy indicator of what is to come later in the morning.

Traders watch futures intently at the time of major economic news releases such as the Unemployment Report, released on the first Friday of each month. Since most important economic news is released at 8:30 A.M. EST, and trading in financial instruments opens at 8:20 EST, futures market action is an excellent indicator of how traders received the news.

FUTURES MARKET QUOTES ON THE CBOT

Source: CBOT.com

Price: Free

FIGURE 3-7

Quotes for the Dow Jones and 30-Year Bond Contracts from CBOT

10 Minute Delayed Snapshot of Futures Quotes
Jul 7, 2000 10:10 am CST - Daytime

CBOT® DJIA^{sm}

	00Sep	00Dec
Opening	10610 10615 7:20 am	10755 7:26 am
Composite High/Low	10724 10:02 am 10610 7:20 am	b 10855 10:02 am 10755 7:26 am
Last 3	10710 10:09 am	b 10845 9:59 am
Last 2	10715 10:09 am	b 10850 10:00 am
Last 1	10720 10:10 am	b 10855 10:02 am
Net Chg	+127	+115
Prv Setl	10593	10740
High/Low Limits	9850	9997
	00Sep	00Dec

10 Minute Delayed Snapshot of Futures Quotes
Jul 7, 2000 10:10 am CST - Daytime

30 Year U.S. Treasury Bonds

	00Sep	00Dec
Opening	9707 9706 7:20 am	9707 7:23 am
Composite High/Low	9802 10:05 am 9706 7:20 am	9731 10:05 am 9706 7:24 am
Last 3	9731 10:09 am	9729 9:58 am
Last 2	9730 10:10 am	9730 10:04 am
Last 1	9731 10:10 am	9731 10:05 am
Net Chg	+25	+26
Prv Setl	9706	9705
High/Low Limits	10006 9406	10005 9405
	00Sep	00Dec

CHAPTER 3 Current Market Prices

Although the CBOT started as a grain exchange over 150 years ago, it was the first to create a financial futures contract. Its financial instruments are now extremely successful, particularly its 5- and 10-year note futures contracts, its 30-year bond contract, and its Dow Jones index contract.

The CBOT's site includes numerous links to additional information and features, including intraday charting. The CBOT restricts dissemination of its quotes on a real-time basis if a fee is not paid to the exchange: note that the two quotes shown have a 10-minute delay.

It's important to know the rules for delivery of futures contracts before trading in them. The bond quote shows that the bond contract trades in terms of price: the 9731 last trade for the Sep 2000 contract is 97 31/32. Therefore, a rally in bonds implies a decrease in yields.

The price of the bond contract is nominally based on a bond with a 6 percent coupon and 20-year maturity. But this price cannot be easily converted to an exact change in yield, because the exchange allows delivery of several different bonds in order to prevent squeezes. Therefore, the delivery rules are mathematically complex. Nevertheless, it is generally true that the change in price of a longer-maturity instrument (e.g., the 30-year bond) will be greater than that of a shorter-maturity instrument (e.g., the 10-year note), for the same change in yield.

QUOTES FOR OPTIONS ON FUTURES ON THE CBOT

Source: TradeSignals.com

Price: Free

FIGURE 3-8

Quotes on Treasury Bond Options from TradeSignals

Welcome to the Tradesignals.com FREE Option Strips service. Please enter a symbol and click the **Get Option** button below. **Click here** for a symbols list.

	Strike	Last	Change	Open	High	Low	Settle	Prev. Close
Put	100-00	3-05	0-00	0-00	0-00	0-00	0-00	3-09
Call	100-00	0-30	0-08	0-24	0-34	0-34	0-00	0-22
Put	102-00	4-57	0-00	0-00	0-00	0-00	0-00	4-57
Call	102-00	–	–	–	–	–	–	–
Put	104-00	6-52	0-00	0-00	0-00	0-00	0-00	6-52
Call	104-00	–	–	–	–	–	–	–
Put	106-00	8-52	0-00	0-00	0-00	0-00	0-00	8-52
Call	106-00	–	–	–	–	–	–	–

September US Treasury Bond Options

TradeSignals.com provides quotes on the highly liquid market in options on futures. In the options-on-futures market, the contract calls for delivery of a futures contract rather than a physical security. Options for each instrument are traded in a different pit from that of the underlying instrument, but the two are in close physical proximity to allow the options *locals* (members who trade for their own accounts) to arbitrage between the instruments.

For the bond options above, trading is in 64ths of a point: for example, the 4-57 quote for the September 102 Puts is 4 57/64.

CHAPTER 3 Current Market Prices

The "September" description of the option refers to delivery of the September futures contract, and not to the expiration date. In fact, expiration is instead seven business days before the first notice day for delivery of the contract, which is two business days before the first business day in the delivery month. For example, the first notice day for the Sep bond contract is late in August, putting expiration of the Sep options in the middle of August.

CUSTOMIZING A COMMODITY WATCH SCREEN

Source: TradeSignals.com

Price: Free

FIGURE 3–9

Customized Commodity Watch Screen from TradeSignals

Refresh this page every 10 minutes automatically   You can still select 9 contracts   **Add Contract**

Contract (click for chart)	Option Strip	Last	Change	Open	High	Low	Settle	Time ET	Prev. Settle 2000-07-06	Prev. Vol 2000-07-06	Prev. OI	Delete
DJU0	Options	10735	142	10610	10740	10610	0	11:39:00	10593	10594	11523	Delete
NDU0	Options	3928	94	3855	3932	3830	0	11:39:00	3834	19430	28251	Delete
SPU0	Options	1497.5	23.8	1478	1498	1476.5	0	11:39:00	1473.7	57354	364591	Delete
TYU0	Options	99-030	1	98-200	99-080	98-200	0	11:38:00	98-175	85730	607620	Delete
USU0	Options	97-27	0--21	97-07	98-02	97-06	0	11:39:00	97-06	135833	372822	Delete
HOU0	Options	0.788	0.003500	0.788	0.7885	0.78	0	11:18:00	0.7845	6236	15606	Delete
JYU0	Options	0.009391	0.000035	0.009421	0.00944	0.009384	0	11:39:00	0.009426	14373	45617	Delete

TradeSignal.com's "Custom Page" allows a trader to program a page to display the trader's choice of commodity contracts. For example, this screen shows the Dow Jones contract (DJ), a Nasdaq contract (ND), an S&P contract (SP), the 10-year note (TY) and 30-year bond (US) contracts, the Heating Oil (HO) contract, and the Japanese yen (JY) contract (the U0 at the end of each contract is code for September 2000). The screen updates automatically every 10 minutes, and the trader can easily link to a chart of the instrument or quotes on its options.

The prices on this date (July 7, 2000) followed a particularly bullish employment report. Note that the bond contract is up

CHAPTER 3 Current Market Prices

21/32, while the shorter-maturity 10-year note contract is up a full point (32/32). This implies that yields for the 10-year sector have declined much more than those of the 30-year sector, because the same change in yield will move the price of a 30-year instrument roughly twice that of a 10-year instrument.

QUOTES ON LISTED STOCK OPTIONS

Source: Quote.com

Price: Free and Premium

FIGURE 3-10

Quotes for Options on Sprint Corp. from Quote

Symbol (Search) FON   Listed   Call   All Strike Prices   Detailed   Frame View   Chain

A|B|C|D|E|F|G|H|I|J|K|L|M|N|O|P|Q|R|S|T|U|V|W|X|Y|Z| INDEX

Delayed
Wednesday July 5 2000, 07/05/2000 11:21:53 AM EST
Sprint Corp   Move the Frame down to see the latest quotes on FON.

Symbol	FON	Net % Change	-0.57
Company Name	Sprint Corp	High	54 $^{13}/_{16}$
Exchange	NYSE	Low	53 $^{3}/_{4}$
Dividend	0.50	Last	54 $^{1}/_{8}$
Market Capitalization	47446.5	Volume	1,582,100
Shares Outstanding	876.61	Tick Volume	782

Delayed
Call Options on FON

Symbol	Month	Strike	High	Low	Last	Volume	OI	Bid	Ask	Net %	Time Value	Intrinsic Value	Days Before Expiration
FONGL	July	60	$^{13}/_{16}$	$^{13}/_{16}$	$^{13}/_{16}$	2	6,064	$^{5}/_{8}$	$^{7}/_{8}$	-18.75	0.81	0.00	16
FONGK	July	55	2 $^{9}/_{16}$	2 $^{9}/_{16}$	2 $^{9}/_{16}$	42	2,244	2	2 $^{3}/_{8}$	+7.89	2.56	0.00	16
FONHL	August	60	1 $^{15}/_{16}$	1 $^{15}/_{16}$	1 $^{15}/_{16}$	37	2,614	1 $^{3}/_{4}$	2	-6.06	1.94	0.00	44
FONHK	August	55	4 $^{1}/_{8}$	3 $^{1}/_{2}$	3 $^{3}/_{4}$	120	4,062	3 $^{3}/_{8}$	3 $^{3}/_{4}$	+3.44	3.75	0.00	44
FONHJ	August	50	6 $^{5}/_{8}$	6	6	202	267	6	6 $^{1}/_{2}$	-4.00	1.88	4.13	44
FONKL	November	60	4 $^{1}/_{2}$	4 $^{1}/_{2}$	4 $^{1}/_{2}$	4	1,191	4 $^{1}/_{8}$	4 $^{1}/_{2}$	+2.85	4.50	0.00	135
FONKK	November	55	6 $^{3}/_{4}$	6 $^{3}/_{4}$	6 $^{3}/_{4}$	60	3,914	6 $^{1}/_{8}$	6 $^{1}/_{2}$	+8.00	6.75	0.00	135
FONKJ	November	50	9 $^{3}/_{8}$	9 $^{3}/_{8}$	9 $^{3}/_{8}$	6	385	8 $^{5}/_{8}$	9 $^{1}/_{8}$	+11.94	5.25	4.13	135
FONAU	January 37 $^{1}/_{2}$		18 $^{7}/_{8}$	18 $^{7}/_{8}$	18 $^{7}/_{8}$	10	1,239	18 $^{1}/_{2}$	19	+6.33	2.25	16.63	198
FONGN	July	70	N/A	N/A	$^{1}/_{4}$	0	2,130	$^{1}/_{16}$	$^{5}/_{16}$	0.00	0.25	0.00	16
FONGM	July	65	N/A	N/A	$^{3}/_{8}$	0	3,087	$^{5}/_{16}$	$^{1}/_{2}$	0.00	0.38	0.00	16
FONGJ	July	50	N/A	N/A	5 $^{5}/_{8}$	0	2,061	5	5 $^{1}/_{2}$	0.00	1.50	4.13	16
FONGI	July	45	N/A	N/A	7 $^{3}/_{4}$	0	12	9 $^{1}/_{4}$	9 $^{3}/_{4}$	0.00	-1.38	9.13	16

CHAPTER 3 Current Market Prices

Quote.com allows the user to display detailed information about listed options. Exchange-traded options have fixed *strike prices* (the price at which the owner of a call has the right to buy the stock, or the owner of a put has the right to sell the stock) and *expiration dates* (the last date on which the option owner may exercise his or her right). The price of the option is the fee or *premium* the option buyer pays for this right.

Volume and *open interest* (the total number of contracts outstanding) are expressed in contracts, where each contract represents 100 shares of the stock. For example, the open interest in the July 60 Call for FON is 6064, which represents the right to buy 606,400 shares of Sprint Corp.

Quote.com conveniently breaks out the two components of the price of an option: its *intrinsic value* (the difference between the current market price and the strike price for in-the-money options) and its *time value* (the value of the probability that the option may become in-the-money or further in-the-money by the expiration date).

The value of an out-of-the-money option is all time value, while the value of a very deep in-the-money option is all intrinsic value. For example, with FON having last traded at 54 1/8 and its August 50 Call having last traded at 6, the August 50 Call is 4.13 points in-the-money [54.125 − 50.00 = 4.125], so its intrinsic value is 4.44 and its time value is 1.88 [6.00 − 4.125 = 1.875]. Quote.com also calculates the number of days to expiration for each option. All else being equal, the value of an option is subject to *time decay*: that is, its time value deteriorates as the time left for the stock to move declines. Time value for an *at-the-money* option (one for which the strike price is equal to the current market price) changes at a rate equal to the square root of time: For example, a stock with four days until expiration will have twice (the square root of 4 is 2) the time value of one with only one day to expiration.

In general, most of any option's daily volume will cluster near the current market price, but this may not be true of open interest. There may be sizable open interest in a strike away from the current market price if, for instance, the price used to be much higher or lower than it is today for a prolonged period of time. Or, traders may be betting on a large move in one direction or another due to a potential trigger event before the expiration date. For example, in the case of Sprint, regulators had recently rejected a previously announced merger with WorldCom for competitive reasons.

Professional traders closely watch the open interest and price action in the options markets. The prices that traders are willing to pay for calls or puts provides more information about their forecasts for the stock than does a simple buy or sell order in the underlying security.

For example, a trader buying a July 60 Call is implicitly predicting that there is a reasonable chance that Sprint will be trading at that price by the expiration date. And by preferring to buy August 60 Calls, the trader is instead predicting that Sprint will take an additional month to reach that price.

Professional traders are also very aware of the effect options markets have on the price of the underlying security at the time of expiration. Assume that on the July expiration date, the price of Sprint suddenly trades from 58 to 60 1/2. At that price, traders short July 60 calls outstanding will have their options unexpectedly exercised, causing them to sell 606,400

CHAPTER 3   Current Market Prices   **41**

shares of Sprint in a rising market. In order to cut their losses and limit their risk, a good number of them will scramble to cover their shorts, driving the price up even further.

The greater the open interest in the option, the greater the potential for such a spike in price. For this reason, traders understand that they may see high volatility on options expiration dates, particularly at the "triple witching hour," when stock index futures contracts, options on the stock index futures, and stock options expire on the same date.

CHAPTER 4

Market Color and Flow

Traders are masters at multitasking. An experienced trader can watch every tick on several securities, execute a trade over the phone, and listen to inquiries and trades on the trading floor and over the squawk box, all at the same time.

During the day, the squawk box carries nearly continuous commentary by support staff, requests by salespeople for bids or offers, and traders showing their "axes" (short for "ax to grind," or a transaction that the trader wants to execute, preferably with one of the firm's customers at a favorable price).

When traders refer to *color* and *flow*, they're imparting information about the nature of market participants with an "ax." Color and flow are especially critical to market makers. For example, no institutional salesperson is allowed to ask a market maker for a bid or offer for his or her customer without revealing the name of the customer, its estimated total size, and very possibly the price that will consummate the trade.

Although such information helps protect the market maker from bidding or offering badly, it serves the more important purpose of assisting all traders at the firm in gauging current buy and sell pressure. One senior sales manager used to always say, "the information is as good as the trade." He meant that it was less important for the market maker to make a fraction of a point on the trade than for the firm to use the information it could derive from the interaction. For this reason, most customer inquiries are relayed to the trader over loudspeakers for all to hear.

The market maker or a *proprietary trader* (a trader with no market-making responsibilities) at the firm could use that information to profit from speculative positions. Or the trading manager might use it to keep the desk out of trouble when something just doesn't smell right.

Consider the case of an options trader who observes selling in put options on the CBOE. If the seller is a well-capitalized arbitrageur who generally takes large positions in attempts to profit from small inefficiencies in the options, the seller's actions are likely to keep the markets in the stock and its options in equilibrium. However, if the selling in the puts comes from many small investors raising cash to meet margin calls, such action may start a chain reaction that drives the price of the underlying stock lower.

Of course, individual investors are not privy to trading room conversations. But professional traders are not privy to most of what they don't see firsthand, either. Instead, they watch the manner in which bids, offers, and size lead to a transaction. For example, when a trade occurs, did the bidder pay up, or did a new lower offer come in the market? And after the trade, was there more for sale on the offer, or was the next offer higher?

From such flow, the skilled trader can attempt to read the minds of traders who can be perceived only as numbers on a screen.

CHAPTER 4 Market Color and Flow

MONITORING FLOW ON THE NYSE AND THE NASDAQ

WindowOnWallStreet.com

Price: Premium

FIGURE 4-1

LiveChart Price History for a Nasdaq-Listed Security from Quote

Quote.com's "LiveChart" feature shows consolidated price history and flow information. Depending on whether the security is listed on the NYSE/Amex or is traded on the Nasdaq, the specific trade details given in the Time and Sales window vary. (A trader can identify a Nasdaq stock by the four characters in its ticker symbol.)

Figure 4–1 shows the LiveChart screen for Nasdaq-listed Lycos (LCOS). The screen includes a 10-minute bar chart spanning two days of trading, as well as Quote.com's Time & Sales book. Strictly speaking, Time & Sales is a recap of previous trades. But Quote.com's version also includes new bids and offers entering the book, depth on the bid or offer, and notice of special conditions such as a sudden order influx, a trading halt for news dissemination, and more.

Note that in this example the downtick indication for the trade at 13:13:31 shows that most traders are legally restricted from selling short at a price of 47 1/4. They are forced to wait for the subsequent uptick at 47 5/16 before they can sell short at that price or higher. If a new seller were to appear at that price, that flow might indicate very bearish sentiment on his part.

FIGURE 4–2

LiveChart Price History for a NYSE-Listed Security from Quote

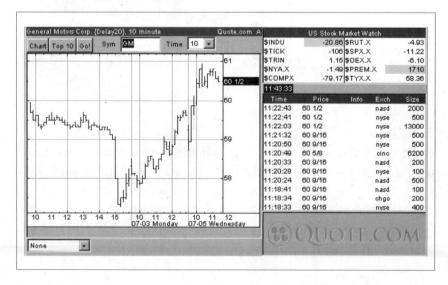

CHAPTER 4 Market Color and Flow   47

Figure 4–2 shows the LiveChart screen for NYSE-listed General Motors (GM). Note that less depth of information is available, because the specialist on the floor does not disseminate all information on bids and offers as he receives them.

FLOW OVER TIME

Source: 3DStockCharts.com

Price: Free

FIGURE 4-3

Three-Dimensional Chart of Cisco from 3DStockCharts

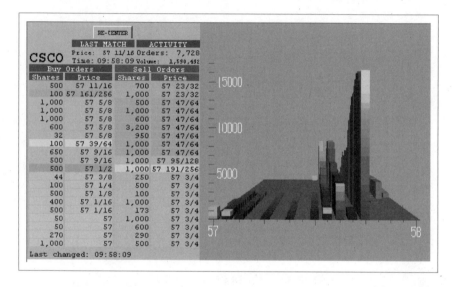

3DStockCharts.com allows a trader to view not only a current snapshot of the bid/offer book, but to view how flow has changed over the last few seconds. This extra insight gives the trader an instantaneous read on the direction of a very short-term trend.

Like the 2D version shown in Figure 3-5, the 3D version shows aggregate size grouped within price bins (in this case, the bins are 1/16 of a point wide) as a function of price. But going backward from the front of the chart, the3DStockCharts display shows that same information for the very recent past, updating about once every half second.

From the chart, it appears that size on the offer has quickly built from under 5000 shares to about 17,000 shares at the 67 3/4 level. At the same time, the size on the bid at the 57 9/16 level has just as quickly evaporated to nearly nothing. This combination strongly indicates that the sellers are dominant at this moment, and that a potential buyer might either bid low or bide his time on his execution.

The tabular display of the order book is useful, as well. Note that much of the offer size that rounds to the 57 3/4 price is actually at a price of 57 47/64. This is an indication that these offers are likely from professionals; individual investors don't usually fine-tune their prices so exactly, preferring to enter orders at rounder fractions such as the 5/8 on the bid. This adds weight to the argument that the sellers will be dominant, at least for the next few minutes.

GRAPHIC STATISTICS FOR FLOW OVER TIME

Source: FalconEye.com

Price: Premium

FIGURE 4-4

Nasdaq Order Book and Chart for Exodus as of July 21, 2000, from FalconEye

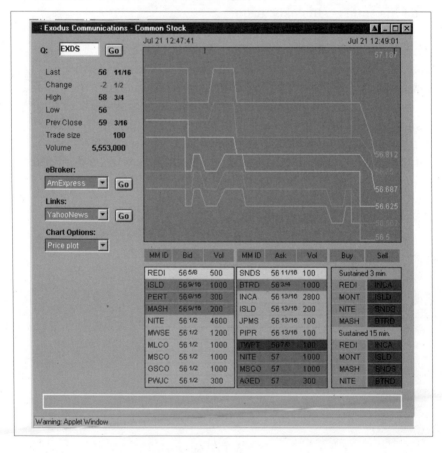

CHAPTER 4 Market Color and Flow

FalconEye is a product of Tachyon Systems: a firm founded by former officers of Goldman Sachs and Bear, Stearns together with the former head of the Soviet Space Research Institute Laboratory. FalconEye makes the daunting task of monitoring all 6500 Nasdaq stocks in real time manageable.

Nasdaq's Level II data feed includes the price, size, and identity of each bid and offer submitted by Nasdaq market makers, including ECNs. Figure 4–4 shows both a tabular and graphic display of that order flow for Exodus Communications. The user can set the type of chart options desired. In this case, the chart displays the changes in price of the major blocks at a price (demarcated by tints) shown in the bid/offer book. The display also shows which market makers have had the largest sustained ax in the security on the bid and the offer side of the market in Exodus. The ranking is determined by a size-weighted moving average over either 3 or 15 minutes.

FalconEye's designers see the ability to search the entire universe of stocks—instead of searching one stock at a time—as one of the system's major advantages. FalconEye allows the user to obtain its Market for 50+ Nasdaq market makers, including all the ECNs.

For example, Figure 4–5 shows its Market Sleuth report, which identifies those stocks for which Morgan Stanley Dean Witter (market maker code MCSO) has notable buy and sell interest at one point in time. (The numbers shown after the stock tickers are a statistical measure of the strength of the ax.) Because Morgan Stanley is known for executing for large institutional investors, its activities can reveal axes of major fund managers.

FIGURE 4-5

Market Sleuth for Morgan Stanley Dean Witter as of July 21, 2000, from FalconEye

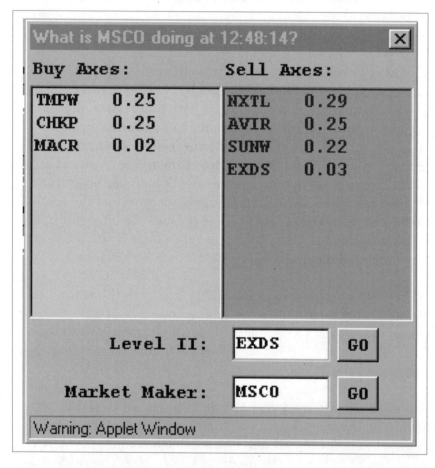

AUTOMATING LIMIT ORDER CALCULATION

Source: FalconEye.com

Price: Premium

FIGURE 4-6

Order Optimizer for Microsoft from FalconEye

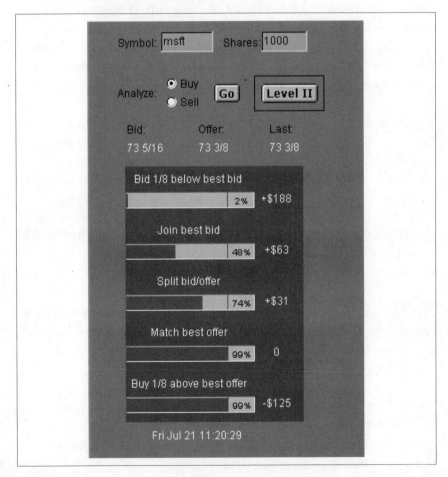

Over 60 percent of the orders entered by individual investors are market orders, but many of these could have been filled at a better price if entered as a limit order instead. Because the founders of FalconEye have trading experience, they recognize the value of optimal limit order entry. FalconEye's "Order Optimizer" assists the trader in deciding at what price to enter a limit order.

Order Optimizer is designed for the individual investor who executes just a few trades a month. Those who do trade much more should develop the skills to enter limit orders themselves, while those who trade much less will not gain much from price improvement on just a few trades.

Figure 4–6 analyzes a buy order for 1000 shares of Microsoft. Based on the real-time history of the last few minutes, the model estimates the probability of execution at several prices. Note that the probability of execution on the offer side is 99 percent—it's not 100 percent because there is a small chance that the offer might be lifted or pulled before the investor can get filled. Conversely, the chance of buying Microsoft 1/8 lower than the bid side is only 2 percent: new selling has to enter the market to execute at that price.

The best bet for an investor who is willing to chance a failure to execute on the offer side is matching the best bid: the chance of execution is 48 percent, and the price improvement over a market order is $63.

The gain from using limit orders on a stock more illiquid than Microsoft could be much greater. In any event, this analysis shows that brokers' commission rates are far less important than their execution capabilities.

CHAPTER 4 Market Color and Flow

DERIVING FUTURE EXPECTATIONS FOR INTEREST RATES

Source: Bloomberg.com

Price: Free

FIGURE 4-7

U.S. Treasury Yield Curve: One-Day Change from Bloomberg

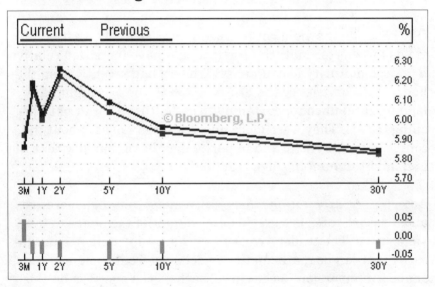

Michael Bloomberg is one of the founders of modern information systems. Nearly every trader has access to a Bloomberg terminal, which provides him with massive amounts of price data, history, and technical analyses for the most esoteric securities over direct phone lines. The full Bloomberg system is expensive: over $1000 per month for the first terminal. However, Bloomberg also offers a free Internet site available to all.

One of Bloomberg's historic strengths is the quality of its information about the interest rates. Fixed-income traders continuously monitor the shape of the *yield curve* (a graph of yield as a function of maturity) for assistance in monitoring changes in expectations about rates. Figure 4–7 shows the shape of the yield curve on July 5 and at the end of the previous day. Each of the *x*-axis points is one of the maturities periodically auctioned by the Treasury: 3-, 6-, and 12-month bills; 2-, 5-, and 10-year notes; and 30-year bonds. The lower graph shows the one-day change in yield for each of these "on-the-run" Treasuries.

On this date, the yield curve has *inverted* severely: that is, yields for shorter-maturity instruments have increased relative to longer-maturity instruments. Traders had recently seen the Federal Reserve leave the *Fed funds rate* (the overnight bank lending rate) unchanged, temporarily halting a series of tightening moves. They were more uncertain than usual about the course of future rates, and in particular the probability that the Fed might tighten in August 2000.

According to *expectations theory*, investors' consensus forecast about future rates is the sole determinant of the shape of the yield curve. The traders' consensus change in opinion about future rates can be mathematically deduced from a change in its shape. An inversion in the curve, such as the one seen on this day, implies that traders have revised their expectation for future rates upward.

In this example, the three-month rate went up about 8 basis points (0.08 percent) and the six-month rate went down about 5 basis points (0.05 percent). This means that on average, Treasury traders expect that three-month rates three months hence will be much lower than they were yesterday.

For instance, assume that a portfolio manager has cash to invest in the Treasury market for six months. The manager has two choices: (1) to invest the cash today for three months at the three-month rate and then reinvest the proceeds for three months hence at the then prevailing rate, or (2) to lock up the cash at the six-month rate today. Theoretically, both investments must produce the same amount of cash at the end of six months, or there is an opportunity for arbitrage.

We can demonstrate the calculation that fixed-income traders perform using the rates of the example:

3-month rate yesterday =	6-month rate yesterday =
5.88 percent	6.22 percent
3-month rate today =	6-month rate today =
5.97 percent	6.18 percent

At yesterday's rates, an investment of $1.00 in six-month bills today will grow to $1.0311 at the end of six months (1 + 6.22 percent × 6/12 = 1.0311). And, an investment of that same $1.00 in a three-month bill today will grow to $1.0147 (1 + 5.88 percent × 3/12 = 1.0147), which will then be reinvested for three months at the unknown forward three-month rate r. Setting the proceeds of each alternate investment equal to each other and solving[1] for r:

$$(1 + 6.22\% \times 6/12) = (1 + 5.88\% \times 3/12) \times (1 + r \times 3/12)$$
$$r = 6.46\%$$

Performing the same calculation using today's rates, we get an implied forward rate of 6.30 percent.

---

[1] This calculation is slightly simplified for illustrative purposes.

Note that, although the current three-month bill rate *rose* 9 basis points (5.97 percent − 5.88 percent = 0.09 percent), the implied forward three-month rate *fell* 16 basis points (6.46 percent − 6.30 percent = 0.16 percent). Traders implicitly forecast that the probability of an increase in short-term rates had just decreased substantially.

As it turns out, this was an accurate forecast. The unemployment report released two days later showed that the economy appeared to be slowing, and yields dropped across the curve.

It is not abnormal for price action to be very different as a function of maturity. Often, when rates move in opposite directions at the two ends of the curve, the curve movement indicates that traders approve or disapprove of expected Fed actions. For example, if traders believe that decisive Fed tightening action is just the medicine the economy needs to halt future inflation, even a Fed tightening that causes short-term rates to *rise* may induce traders to buy bonds and cause long-term rates to *fall*.

CHAPTER 4 Market Color and Flow

IDENTIFYING ORDER IMBALANCES ON A REAL-TIME BASIS

Source: Quotezart.com

Price: Free

FIGURE 4-8

Musical Quotes for Nasdaq Stocks on Island from Quotezart

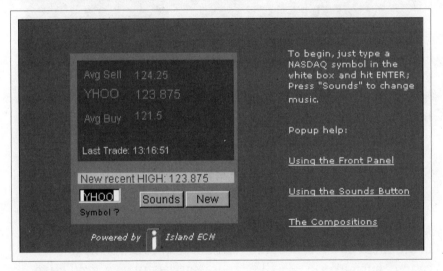

Quotezart.com urges its users to "Listen to the markets! Hear your stocks move!" Quotezart sets real-time changes in price to music. Although this audio format will be no more than a novelty to most traders, some might appreciate sound cues for key events.

More useful is Quotezart's real-time calculation of the average prices of all buy orders and sell orders in Island's electronic

FIGURE 4-9

Buy/Sell Ratio for Nasdaq Stocks on Island from Quotezart

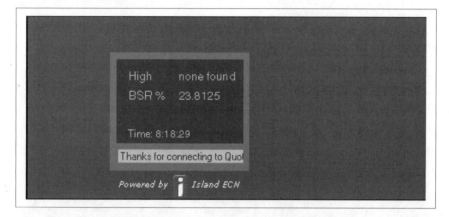

book as can be seen in Figure 4–8. Quotezart color-codes the average prices displayed.

For example, if the average price of sell orders has just increased, it's shown in green. So, theoretically, if both the average sell and the average buy are shown in green, buy orders may be coming in at higher prices, lower sell prices are either being filled or cancelled, and market flow is to the upside. Of course, such averages will be more successful as a predictive device for stocks in which Island is particularly active, such as technology and Internet stocks.

Quotezart has also created its proprietary *BSR percent* indicator, which is the simple ratio of the total number of buy orders divided by the total number of sell orders at any given time for *all* the Nasdaq securities in the Island electronic book. According to Quotezart, BSR percent acts as an oscillator, tending to fluctuate between 30 and 55 percent or so, and may foretell short-term moves in the Nasdaq. The indicator is updated about every seven seconds, and is also available in chart form. Quotezart is monitoring the usefulness of changes in BSR percent as a leading indicator of market action.

Traders might also use BSR percent as an early morning indicator of the day to come. The snapshot of Figure 4–9 was taken at 8:19 A.M. EST on July 5, 2000. Early morning trading was active, because Computer Associates had released an earnings warning on the evening of July 3 when markets were closed for the Fourth of July holiday. The BSR percent of 23.8 percent is extraordinarily low, but indications for Nasdaq futures were down only about 40 points. The intraday chart for the Nasdaq on July 5 shown in Figure 2–1 shows the aftermath. The Nasdaq closed down well over 100 points that day.

Although Quotezart does not weight the individual securities in creating its indices, traders must be aware that there is an implicit weighting toward those securities for which Island has the deepest books (most orders). Therefore, one would expect it to be more volatile and less reliable for classes of securities in which Island is not active, or at times of the day when the markets are thin.

MONITORING INSTITUTIONAL INTEREST MESSAGES

Source: ThomsonInvest.net

Price: Free and Premium

FIGURE 4-10

Institutional Activity for Nokia from Thomson

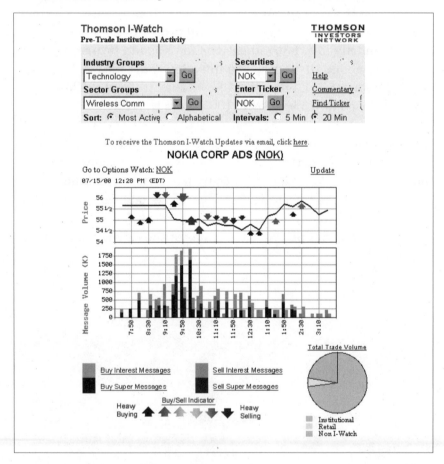

CHAPTER 4 Market Color and Flow

The "I-Watch" feature from Thomson Real Time Quotes captures and summarizes institutional *interest messages*, that is, messages from broker/dealers to their institutional clients (generally, fund managers).

These messages take one of two forms. A plain-vanilla buy or sell interest message indicates that a broker/dealer has an "ax-to-grind" or a particular interest in buying or selling a particular security, and solicits further discussion as to price and size. Or, a *super-interest message* bids or offers specific size and price, and can be traded on, at least for a few seconds. Super-interest messages are used only for blocks of at least 25,000 shares, and are therefore a more important indicator of institutional activity.

Thomson allows a trader to create this report for a specific industry group (e.g., Technology), a sector within that group (e.g., Wireless Communications), or a specific stock. Or, the trader can also request the report for just the top ten securities in a group.

In the upper chart of Figure 4–10, Thomson indicates interest messages for Nokia on July 14, 2000, by arrows, separating the super-interest messages from the regular messages. The direction of each arrow indicates the dominance of buy or sell orders, the point of each arrow indicates the weighted average price of the messages, the size of the arrow indicates the relative number of shares, and its color indicates relative strength.

The buy and sell interest information is lagged no more than 10 minutes, and therefore should provide useful flow information to a trader, especially since buy and sell messages seem to occur in *runs*: that is, several observations in the same direction.

In the lower chart of Figure 4–10, Thomson summarizes total message volume in bar chart form, again broken out by type of interest. Note that the peak of message volume occurs near opening time for the floor-based exchanges. Thomson allows the user to set the bin width to 5 minutes or 20 minutes. Near the open, 5-minute bars would provide more information about developing order flow.

Thomson also breaks out total trade volume in a pie chart at the bottom of each report. Thomson collects its data from those brokers who report back to Thomson's proprietary communications network. This reporting is voluntary, so total trade volume does not include every transaction.

Whether Thomson flags a trade as institutional or retail is a function of who reported the trade. If it was reported by a broker who primarily executes for retail accounts (such as Charles Schwab's Mayer Schweitzer), the trade will be flagged as retail. If it was reported by a large brokerage firm known primarily for covering fund managers, the trade will be flagged as institutional.

Figure 4–11 shows the Thomson message report late on July 15, 2000. Just before the close of trading, a Florida jury ordered the tobacco industry to pay $145 billion in punitive damages to 500,000 Florida smokers.

The interest arrows show that this event was a case of "sell on the rumor, buy on the fact." The price of Philip Morris—expected to be the worst hit by such judgments—had already fallen about 10 percent that week. Because the worst was out of the way, some traders felt that it was now less risky to bet that the judgment would be overturned during the forthcoming years of appeals. As the buy interest at the end of the day shows, some institutional buyers were willing to buy the stock at cheaper levels.

CHAPTER 4 Market Color and Flow 65

FIGURE 4-11

Institutional Activity for Philip Morris from Thomson

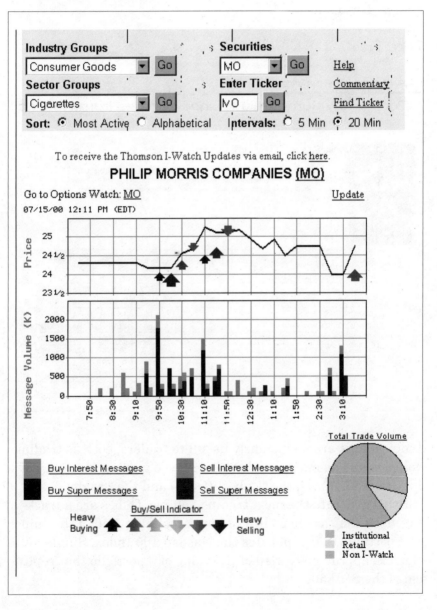

COMPARING INDEX SHARES

Source: Nasdaq.com

Price: Free

FIGURE 4-12
Price and Volume Data for Index Shares from Nasdaq

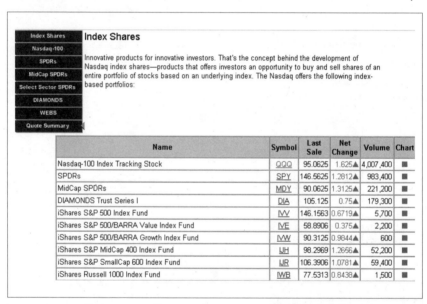

Index shares are particularly useful to traders, both as trading vehicles and as market indicators. As the trading summary of Figure 4-12 shows, the "Cubes" (QQQ) and the "Spiders" (SPDR) generate the most trading volume. Cubes are a tracking stock that has been priced to approximate 1/40 of the value of a portfolio that replicates the Nasdaq-100 Index. Similarly, Spiders approximate 1/10 of the value of a portfolio that replicates the S&P 500 Index.

Unlike a calculated index, these tracking stocks can be traded directly. As a result, they reflect traders' opinions more exactly and quickly. Unlike most stocks, they are exempt from the downtick rule that prohibits new short selling on downticks. So, index stocks might be the first choice of a short-seller who wants to bet on a general market decline, which might make these stocks more responsive to bearish sentiment.

MONITORING COMMODITY PRICES

Source: Bloomberg.com

Price: Free

FIGURE 4-13

Commodity Movers from Bloomberg

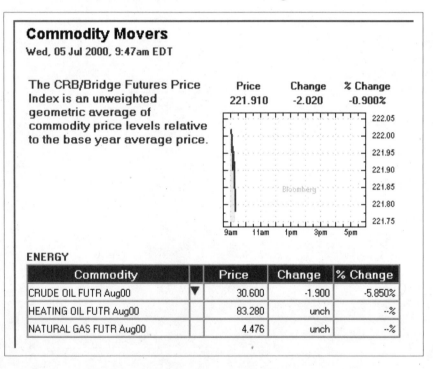

Bloomberg.com's Commodity Movers page provides an intraday chart of the CRB (Commodity Research Board)/Bridge index of commodity futures prices, and provides details about price action in each of its components.

Figure 4–13 displays just the first few lines of the detail following the chart. In addition to energy commodities, the index includes grains, industrials (copper and cotton), livestock, precious metals, and the so-called soft commodities (cocoa, coffee, sugar, and frozen orange juice). Although the choice of commodities may seem a bit eclectic, it's based on those commodities with liquid futures markets.

A substantial change in CRB can sometimes lead a change in interest rates (because commodity prices affect future inflation rates) by seconds or minutes. And, a change in interest rates can often lead a change in stock prices, even in those stocks not directly affected by the commodity or commodities responsible.

But traders need to be aware of which components of the index are responsible for the change in CRB: A change in orange juice prices won't affect many stocks, while a change in oil prices might. And a professional trader will dig deep for the reason behind the commodity price action. For example, on this date (July 5, 2000) OPEC had recently announced a potential increase in oil production. This news was reflected in the price of the August 2000 Crude Oil futures contract, which was down $1.90 for the day.

ANTICIPATING THE TRADING DAY

Source: Nasdaq.com

Price: Free

FIGURE 4-14

Most Active Stocks: Premarket and After Hours from Nasdaq

Nasdaq Most Active — Pre-Market / After Hours
June 30, 2000 - After Hours Market Closed

Total After Hours Share Volume	346,345,300

Nasdaq - After Hours Ten Most Active Share Volume   Advanced   Declined

Company Name / Symbol	Market Close	Last Sale (After Hours)	% Change (After Hours)	Share Volume (After Hours)	Daily News
BROADCOM - BRCM Broadcom Corporation	$218.9375	$218.4375	0.23%	17,911,800	News
CISCO SYSTEMS - CSCO Cisco Systems, Inc.	$63.5625	$63.7344	0.27%	7,416,800	News
Microsoft - MSFT Microsoft Corporation	$80	$79.875	0.16%	4,764,800	News
comcast - CMCSK Comcast Corporation	$40.5	$40.5	NA	3,936,000	News
intel - INTC Intel Corporation	$133.6875	$134.75	0.79%	2,879,200	News
WORLDCOM - WCOM WorldCom, Inc.	$45.875	$45.875	NA	2,649,000	News

The Nasdaq's Web site includes a feature that ranks stocks by highest premarket or after-hours volume.

Many companies release earnings reports, warnings, and other material information outside of normal exchange trading hours in order to prevent market disruptions. They are particularly likely to do so if the news is bad: Computer Associates was widely criticized for issuing an earnings warning and announcing an accounting delay close to midnight on July 3, 2000.

The Nasdaq's site includes links to company news so a trader can identify the source of the volume. In this case, three of the top six stocks by volume are telecommunications companies, and the volume was doubtless due to the rampant takeover speculation at the time involving nearly every big name in the industry.

IDENTIFYING CHART PATTERNS AND TRIGGER LEVELS

Source: BigCharts.com

Price: Free

FIGURE 4–15

Multiday 15-Minute Bar Chart for Broadcom from BigCharts

The most useful tool traders have in identifying trading patterns and making short-term forecasts is the chart. BigCharts.com is another site with excellent charting capabilities, including customizable charts in the open-high-low-close format preferred by most traders. Figure 4–15 shows a chart of Broadcom from the open on Friday, June 30, 2000, to slightly after noon Monday, July 3, or 1 1/2 trading days.

In trading, it's often advantageous to be a contrarian rather than a member of the herd, but this is not usually true in charting. Traders should view charts in the same way other traders do, because important chart points or formations can trigger actions by other traders. For example, traders would consider Monday's 192 1/2 low as a support level. If Broadcom violated that level, traders with long positions might have sell stops triggered, and *technicians* (traders who are primarily motivated by price patterns) might institute fresh short positions.

Traders had warning of Broadcom's potential volatility on Monday. Note that, although Broadcom actually opened lower on July 3, it trended upward for the next three hours. Traders observing Broadcom's after-hours volume on Friday (as Figure 4–14 shows, it was the most active after-hours stock on that date) would have been warned that many traders who couldn't or wouldn't participate in Friday night's activity still had a job to do on Monday.

ANTICIPATING THE NEXT DAY

Source: Quote.com

Price: Free

FIGURE 4-16

Top Stock Options Ranked by Volume from Quote

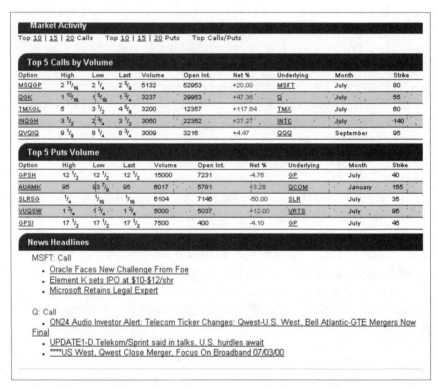

Quote.com displays the most active options, both for Nasdaq and exchange-traded stocks (the Nasdaq stocks all have four characters in their ticker symbols).

The greatest profit for a trader who is very bullish or bearish on a stock will come from buying puts or calls on that stock. The options markets allow the trader to pay just a few dollars per share for the option, rather than paying for the full amount of the stock. Thus there is a greater opportunity for profit, even over a margined stock account, as well as limited downside.

The call or put buyer is making a precision bet: Unless the trader accurately predicts both the *size* and *direction* of future prices, the trader will watch the value of the option decay over time, and the entire investment may be lost. So, a professional options trader who buys an option is "long volatility," that is, the trader is betting that the magnitude of future price moves (either up or down) will be large. Otherwise, if the market traded slightly up, the trader would have been better off owning the underlying stock, and if the market traded slightly down, would have been better off with no position.

Therefore, it's useful to observe not only which stocks underlie the options with highest volume, but, more precisely, which strikes and expiration dates are attracting that volume.

Quote.com conveniently displays the news items related to each of the stocks (Figure 4–16 shows just a partial list), so the trader can determine whether the options market is reacting to old news, acticipating news not yet released, or even reacting to news or rumors not yet fully disseminated.

SPOTTING CHANGES IN VOLATILITY

Source: Optionetics.com

Price: Free and Premium

Optionetics.com specializes in supplying options-related information. Much of this data must be calculated from other market prices, such as the price of the option, the price of the underlying security, and the risk-free interest rate using sophisticated mathematical models.

It's nearly impossible for an options trader to monitor options by watching options prices. For example, it's hard to tell how much of the price increase of a call is due to a price increase in its underlying security, and how much of that increase is due to increased optimism about the chance of future price increases. Further, the price of the call may drop just because time passed: It is subject to time decay because the probability of a large move falls as time to expiration decreases.

Instead, professional traders monitor *implied volatility,* a statistic derived from the price of an option that represents its value. Professional traders think about options in terms of "implied vol" the way traders of other securities think in terms of price. As Figure 4–17 shows, this statistic can be watched from day to day without requiring adjustment for loss of time value or change in the price of the underlying security.

Implied volatility is a measure of the magnitude of expected price moves until expiration. It is calculated by solving for the value for volatility that would statistically imply that the value

FIGURE 4-17

Implied Volatility Chart for Infinity Broadcasting from Optionetics

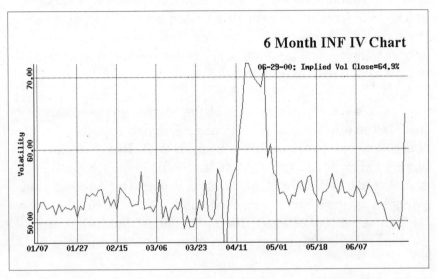

of the option is equal to its current market price. Implied volatility—derived as it is from the market price of the option—is, therefore, a consensus forecast about the magnitude of future price moves.

Implied volatility is forward looking, unlike *historical volatility* (a statistical calculation based on historical prices), which is backward looking.

The normal unit in which volatility is expressed is one standard deviation of the percentage change in the price of the underlying security for one year. For a normal distribution (one formed by a random-walk process), one standard deviation encompasses about 65 percent of all possible price moves. For example, the implied volatility for Infinity Broadcasting is 64.89 percent. This means the market estimates that the price of the stock is 65 percent likely to stay within a +/– 65.89 percent price range over one year. However, that one-year statistic serves to normalize all quotes, regardless of how many days each option has to expiration.

In Figure 4–18, Optionetics identifies stocks whose volatility has broken out from its recent range. Implied volatility can fluctuate from day to day, just as price does. But when it changes significantly relative to its recent history, a professional trader will investigate. In this report, Optionetrics compares an option's current implied volatility to the high and low boundaries of its *Bollinger Bands*: bands around its average implied volatility that generally encompass two standard devi-

FIGURE 4–18

Stock Options Ranked by Breakouts in Implied Volatility from Optionetics

Top	20 day Bollinger Band Implied Volatility Ranking for 06-29-00			
OPTIONS ON THIS END ARE BREAKING OUT HIGHER!				
Stock Option	High	Low	Current	Chg
1) Infinity Broadcasting Corp. (INF)	59.68%	46.38%	64.89%	+13.42%
2) Unisys Corporation (UIS)	100.60%	73.12%	110.26%	+19.44%
3) Andrew Corporation (ANDW)	67.20%	55.15%	71.38%	+10.18%
4) US LEC Corp (CLEC)	120.73%	78.39%	134.18%	+14.37%
5) Xerox Corporation (XRX)	54.23%	41.06%	58.32%	+12.56%
6) CONSOL ENERGY INC (CNX)	66.97%	12.32%	83.78%	+67.60%
7) TOO INC (TOO)	96.22%	58.09%	106.78%	+31.68%
8) Goodyear Tire & Rubber Compan (GT)	46.00%	37.71%	48.23%	+6.20%
9) Huntington Bancshares, Inc. (HBAN)	63.00%	45.59%	67.16%	+14.76%
10) Briggs and Stratton Corporati (BGG)	76.12%	33.36%	84.74%	+8.97%

ations of changes to that volatility. In the case of Infinity Broadcasting, its current implied volatility of 64.89 percent broke through the upper Bollinger Band level of 59.68 percent. Infinity's sudden spike in implied volatility is also shown in the chart of Figure 4–17.

Implied volatility will generally increase for one of four reasons. First, historical volatility may have increased, and the market generally assumes that the future is best represented by the recent past. Second, a scheduled event that may be a source of volatility might be looming on the horizon. For example, the volatility of options on bond futures generally increases before Fed meetings. Third, a recent shock to the price of the underlying security may have just occurred. And fourth, volatility may change as the time to expiration changes. Implied volatility usually goes up as the time to expiration drops, especially when the time to expiration is less than a week or so.

By looking at price history, news, and calendars of upcoming events, a trader can determine which of the four is responsible for a change. A search of news items, a review of price history, and the calendar suggests nothing extraordinary going on in Infinity on June 29. However, just before the open on June 30, the analyst at Thomas Weisel reiterated his "Strong Buy" recommendation and earnings estimates.

LISTENING TO LIVE COLOR

Source: LOS.net

Price: Premium

Listen Only Squawk Box provides the kind of color formerly available only to the largest institutional commodity traders. LOS.net has a commentator on the floor of the Chicago Mercantile Exchange providing live commentary on price, size, and players for S&P 500 futures and Nasdaq futures over the Internet. Traders can hear about a change in the market before they see it on their screens. In addition, they offer the ability to message the pit, ask questions, and request commentary.

Squawkbox.com prides itself on providing users with commentary from the same expert brokers used by top proprietary traders at the largest investment banks; the individual and the professional are both listening to the same commentary in real time.

CHAPTER 5

Price History, Charting, and Pattern Recognition

Professional traders are visually oriented. Most program their screens to display real-time charts that update with every tick in price for key securities. In addition to their own specialties, all traders watch movement in the major stock indices, interest rates, currencies, and key commodity prices such as oil. Experienced traders know that history repeats itself, and the form in which most professional traders choose to view that history is the chart.

If value investing is flying on visual, then technical trading is flying on instruments. Every transaction leaves its footprints for all to see as historical prices. Charting is an exercise in pattern recognition. A trader who can identify the start of a pattern has implicitly forecast the next market move—the part of the pattern that hasn't happened yet.

Traders can rely on charts because, in doing so, they're relying on people being people. The catalysts that dominate market action are the simplest: fear and greed. And the actions humans take in response to those triggers create repetitive and recognizable patterns.

Although few traders are pure *technicians* (those who depend heavily on the interpretation of charts in their trading), most traders believe that charts are often useful as a predictive tool. They use them to identify the optimal entry and exit spots from trades, and to recognize when chart conditions may trigger new orders.

THE INEFFICIENT MARKET HYPOTHESIS

Traders don't accept the theory that the market is *efficient* (that is, all that is known about a security is instantly reflected in its market price). They know that, for a variety of reasons, humans take time to react to new information. Some estimate that prices trend about 30 percent of the time. And it can be shown that there is *serial correlation* (one day's behavior is correlated to that of the previous day) in price changes. For example, one can often observe more up moves in a row (generating an upward trend) than is explained by chance.

These observations are not a statistical anomaly, because they can be explained in terms of human behavior. First, there are external forces that are not random. The Fed might raise interest rates six times in a row, affecting every security in the United States in a systematic way. Or an investor might watch the price of a security degrade for a week before throwing in the towel and entering a new sell order.

Or more simply, the attitudes of both professional traders and individual investors are affected by what happened to their positions the day before: Memory and emotion create serial correlation. And natural selection is at work—the winners stay in the market, the losers leave. Some events are like meteor showers to dinosaurs.

TRADER PSYCHOLOGY AND TRIGGER EVENTS

At times, there are large groups of investors vulnerable to the same stimuli. Assume, for instance, that many individual investors bought a security at a price of 50 and watched it rally before falling back to 51. Falling below breakeven is often a trigger event for an investor. The investor will feel differently about a decline from 51 to 50 than one from 50 to 49. Many owners of that stock are willing to wait the market out as long as the price stays above that level (creating support at 50), but will be quick to liquidate their positions if it should trade below 50 (violating support and spiking downward).

In such a manner, investors acting in concert as they react to trigger events can generate repetitive patterns in prices. However, traders will be most successful if they rely only on the simplest chart patterns. Humans are good at seeing patterns where none exist (as in a Rorschach test), and can often see complex chart formations where none exist. A *double bottom* is obvious; a *head-and-shoulders* formation is not, and will not carry the weight of many traders acting in concert.

UNDERSTANDING THE FOUNDATIONS OF CHARTING

Source: Bridge.com

Price: Free and Premium Services

FIGURE 5-1

Relative Strength with Volume at a Price Chart from Bridge

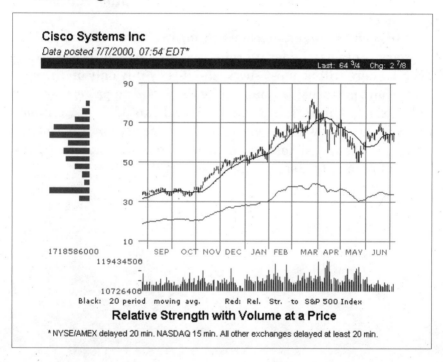

Bridge Data is one of the primary providers of pricing data and market information systems to institutional traders, but it also has a Web site available to the public.

Bridge.com's Relative Strength with Volume at a Price chart assists the trader in two ways.

First, Bridge's Relative Strength chart compares the performance of a single security to the performance of the index it is expected to track. This feature helps a trader determine whether the behavior or the price of a stock is due to its own merits or whether it has just been pulled along by general market action. Bridge determines the appropriate choice of index. For example, the lower line in Figure 5–1 shows that Cisco has been outperforming the S&P 500 index: an index of which it is a member.

Second, Bridge's Volume at a Price indicator helps illustrate the way in which human behavior establishes chart formations. This indicator represents the total volume that traded within a price bin, irrespective of the time at which it occurred. The largest volume for the 10 months shown in the figure occurred at or near a price of 35.

Volume at a Price could be high for one of two reasons. The stock could have traded with moderate volume at that level many times, as it did at a price of 35 or so. Or it could have traded with high volume just a few times, as it did at a price of 70 or so.

In either case, many new positions were instituted at that price, and the cost basis of a new position is a number always in an investor's mind. Humans are not machines, and owners of Cisco are likely to get nervous about their position if the price of Cisco trades back down through their break-even level. When Volume at a Price is high, it means that many people will be feeling similar emotions at the same time. And when people act in concert, prices move.

Although it may not be logical, a trader feels differently about a position that's slightly underwater than one that's slighty profitable. As long as the position is profitable, the trader may hold on longer than is advisable. And when the position turns unprofitable, the trader may liquidate too soon.

Traders who bought Cisco near 70 as a short-term play and saw it trade up 10 points, for example, must have been very nervous when it started approaching 70 again. Note that when the price of Cisco traded back below 60 for the first time, the price spiked downward, very likely because of stop loss orders and other liquidation. Traders say that they want to be "first in the door, but first out of the door": meaning they do not want to be part of a rush for the fire exits when someone yells "Fire!"

CHAPTER 5 Price History, Charting, and Pattern Recognition   87

CONSTRUCTING TREND LINES

Source: CNET.com

Price: Free

FIGURE 5-2

Interactive Java Chart with Trend Lines from CNET

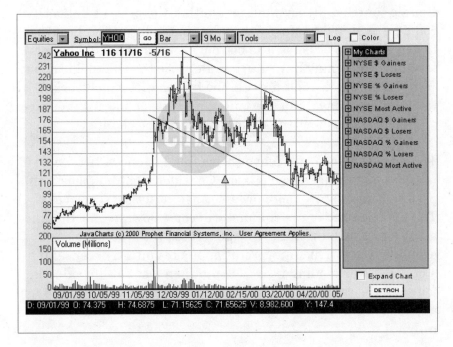

CNET's site is primarily known for information about technology. However, it's also one of the best sites around for information on technology stocks.

CNET provides the trader with the ability to manipulate a chart interactively. In Figure 5-2, note that the two trend lines form a *channel*, or two parallel lines that define a range within which prices are expected to trade. The lines were drawn by pointing and clicking, superseding the old pen-and-ruler method of charting. The channel was drawn in the traditional manner: from highs and lows generated by an OHLC bar chart of daily price action. When looking for long-term trends, daily charts rather than minute charts are more appropriate.

Classic charting theory would state that the price of Yahoo! could be expected to stay within the channel. But if it breaks through the top or below the bottom of the channel, an important new trend may have started. Because the channel is about 80 points wide, it won't provide the trader with much assistance on most days. But the trader must be on alert if the price of Yahoo! trades near the bottom or top of the channel.

The price of Yahoo! can leave the channel in one of two ways: if its price moves, or if time passes. Consider what happens if the price of Yahoo! stays more or less constant for several weeks. The upper bound of the channel will come down to meet it, and a buy signal will eventually be generated if the stock doesn't decline further. This interpretation makes intuitive sense: If a stock that was trading near 250 and then lost half its value in four months can stabilize near its current price of 116 11/16 for any length of time, perhaps it has the potential for another rally.

CHAPTER 5 Price History, Charting, and Pattern Recognition

SELECTING THE APPROPRIATE CHARTING PERIOD

Source: MSN.com

Price: Free

FIGURE 5-3

Year-to-Date Price History for Salton, Inc. from MSN

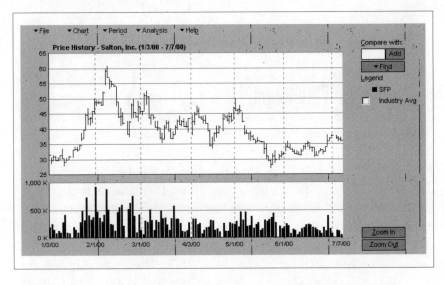

Figures 5-3 and 5-4 show the price of Salton for two different time periods. Figure 5-3 encompasses the longer time period: a year-to-date chart showing six months of data. This chart looks reasonably bullish; Salton appears to have good support at about the 27 1/2 level because of the double bottom at that price. But Figure 5-4 shows only the last three months of data. This chart looks more negative; Salton has retraced over half of its three-month range after making two highs close to 50.

FIGURE 5-4

Three-Month Price History for Salton, Inc. from MSN

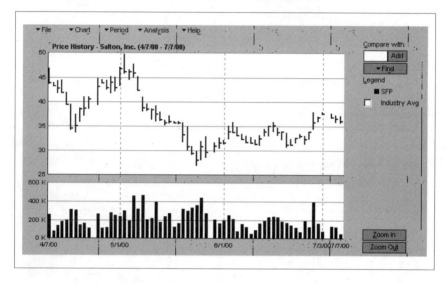

Figures 5-3 and 5-4 illustrate the primary caveat regarding charting: Drawing trend lines and chart formations is a subjective process, and humans often see what they want to see. The chart of Figure 5-2 was set to display nine months of data. But if it had been set to display year-to-date data or two years of data (two other options offered by CNET), the lines might have been drawn very differently. When charting, it's best to look at the data over various time periods, and to rely on only the simplest and most obvious patterns.

CHAPTER 5 Price History, Charting, and Pattern Recognition   91

IDENTIFYING KEY PRICES

Source: CBOT.com

Price: Free

FIGURE 5-5

Intraday Bond Futures Price Chart from CBOT

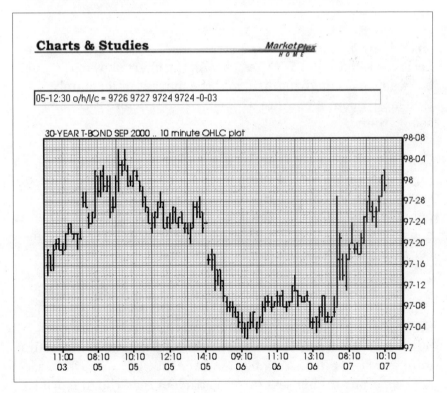

CBOT.com provides a great deal of information about the contracts traded on the floor of the Chicago Board of Trade, and includes a variety of quote and charting options.

Figure 5–5 shows a 10-minute OHLC bar chart of the Sep 2000 bond futures contract from July 3 to midday of July 7. Support and resistance levels are created when traders tend to act in unison at the same price. And speculative traders often rely on short-term charts such as this one to identify entry and exit spots, which then become support and resistance. When attempting to make very short-term forecasts, a chart such as this one, which displays data in bins of just a few minutes, is appropriate.

On Friday, July 7, the all-important employment statistics report was released at 7:30 A.M. CST. As the chart shows, the number was surprisingly bullish, and the market immediately traded up about a point to 97-29 (97 29/32) before retracing some ground.

Consider a trader who carries a speculative position through an important "number" (trader jargon for economic news release) such as this one. Before it's released, the trader must anticipate the price levels at which to liquidate the position, either at a loss or with a profit. There is no time to do so after the number as important as this one.

Even if the trader were on the phone with the trading floor in Chicago, it would not be possible to sell the bonds at 97-28 if the trader waited to see the bond trade at that price before putting in the order. Price action is exceedingly wild in the first minute or two after a number. And the market can turn in seconds as profit-taking sets in, or as traders read the fine print instead of the headlines of the news release and change their opinions.

So, professional traders often put in orders (both profit-taking and loss-limiting) ahead of time, just in case. To identify the

CHAPTER 5   Price History, Charting, and Pattern Recognition   93

best prices for these orders, a trader will turn to the charts to identify both support and resistance.

Assume that the trader has a long position in bond futures, and is analyzing the charts early on the morning of July 7. Above the market, the trader sees that 97-29 was the high trade of the last couple of hours of trading on July 5—a price never reached again on July 6. Above that level was 98-06, the high of July 5.

Depending on how greedy the trader is, sell orders might be entered to take profits at either of these prices. Because liquidation at the lower price is still a very good profit, the trader might either split the order (selling half at each price), or go for the lower price as a bird-in-the-hand.

Below the market, the bond has nearly made a *double bottom* (two lows at the same price, generally considered important support) at 97-02 and 97-03 on July 6. So, the trader would likely place sell stop orders a little below 97-02 to limit the loss if the number were bearish.

As Figure 5–5 shows, the bond traded up to 97-29 immediately after the number. At this point, profit taking entered the market, and sellers without the foresight to place advance orders may have liquidated their positions at worse levels. Later in the day the price made a new high of 98-02, but could not reach the 98-06 resistance level. A contributing factor to the bond's failure to trade higher was that 98-02 is exactly one point above the support level of 97-02, a fact some bond chartists consider significant.

When the price of the bond fell just short of an important resistance level such as 98-08, chartists might have interpreted this to mean that the buying pressure had run out of steam—particularly since it was late in the trading day on a Friday. Speculators might set fresh short positions for the rest of the day, with buy stops above the high. But new buyers would likely wait until Monday to set new positions.

CHAPTER 6

Analytic Indicators and Models

Professional traders often select one or more *analytic indicators* as enhancements to their real-time price displays, that is, indicators intended to provide market predictions. Most of these indicators are calculated solely from price. They are created from rule-based models that generate buy and sell signals in an objective manner. In a sense, "analytics" is quantified charting.

Analytic models generally fall into one of two categories: they attempt to identify the current trend, or provide leading indicators that identify turning points in the trend. Since most traders believe that markets trend at least part of the time, identification of a new trend provides them with an entry signal into a position in which "the trend is your friend." But markets get overbought and oversold as well—the trend represents only a general drift. So other analytic models that attempt to identify the peaks and valleys of price history are understandably popular.

Even those traders who discount the theory behind analytic models must be aware of the conditions when the most popular models might generate a buy or sell signal. If many other traders believe in the methodology, the technique may generate self-fulfilling prophesies, because their new orders will make it so. The Internet has increased the importance of certain indicators. For example, the 50-day and the 200-day moving averages are standard choices on the MSN.com drop-down menu, and traders new to analytic techniques may take on faith that these are key indicators to watch.

CHAPTER 6 Analytic Indicators and Models   97

IDENTIFYING A CHANGE IN TREND

Source: MSN.com

Price: Free

FIGURE 6–1

Salton Chart with Moving Averages from MSN

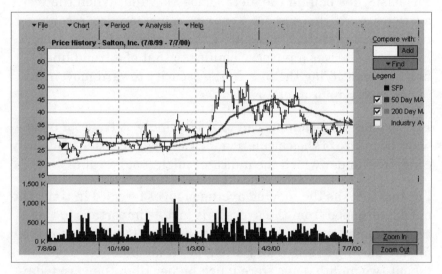

MSN.com provides a very flexible charting capability. The trader can select a chart style, time period, and analytic indicators to be added to the chart. The trader can also compare a security to one or more other securities or indicators.

Figure 6–1 shows the price of Salton, Inc. for the past year, along with the 50-day and 200-day moving averages of its price.

The most basic type of analytic index is the *moving average*, the average price for the last n days plotted on a calendar axis. The moving average crossover technique is probably the oldest of the analytic forecasting models. According to the rules of the model, when the shorter-term moving average crosses through the longer-term moving average, a new trend is established and a buy or sell signal is generated. For example, as shown in Figure 6–1, the 50-day average stayed well above the 200-day moving average until the end of June, keeping a buy signal intact until a sell signal was generated when the lines crossed.

The basic idea behind the methodology is valid. When the two averages cross, this signals a change in momentum: recent activity is more positive or negative than earlier activity. A moving average serves a purpose similar to that of a trend line, namely, identifying the bias in the security toward movement in one direction or another.

But no analytic technique can be used blindly. A trader must always be aware of the calculation methodology in order to identify conditions under which the indicator might not be valid.

For instance, as the moving average moves forward in time, the old day dropped from the average is just as important to the calculation as the new day added to it. If, as is the case for the 50-day moving average for Salton, prices 50 business days (about two months) ago were much higher than they are today, the 50-day moving average will drop unless Salton commences a serious rally. It seems intuitively correct that a buy or sell signal triggered by an analytic technique will be more reliable if current data—rather than past data—triggered the signal. Therefore, this sell signal is suspect.

Further, traders should be aware that a moving average lags the market, and that a moving average crossover technique will rarely indicate a sell signal at highs or a buy signal at lows. To trade by such rules, a trader must have enough capital and staying power to ride out adverse periods.

CHAPTER 6   Analytic Indicators and Models   99

FINDING EXPERT TECHNICAL AIDS

Source: TradeStation.com (see also OmegaResearch.com)

Price: Premium

FIGURE 6-2

Price and RSI Chart of Microsoft from TradeStation

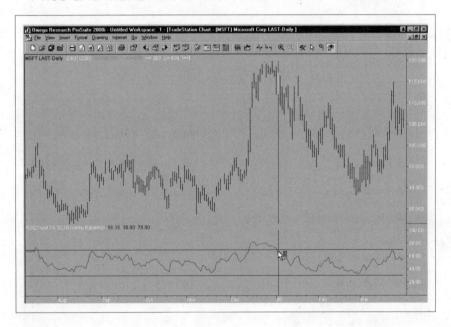

For the trader who wants professional quality analytics, is reasonably computer literate, and is willing to pay what it's worth, ProSuite 2000i from Omega Research is the answer. The trader can use any of three pieces of software: TradeStation, OptionStation, and RadarScreen, which enable monitoring a huge number of analytic measures on a real-time basis.

The TradeStation bar chart of Figure 6–2 shows the price of Microsoft for the second quarter of 2000, while the line shows the value of an RSI indicator. Figure 6–3 shows just a small sample of the analytic possibilities offered by TradeStation. Note that it also provides definitions of each indicator.

One special feature of TradeStation is the expert interpretation it provides about the state of the analytic indicators at any

FIGURE 6-3

Drop-Down Menu of Analysis Techniques from TradeStation

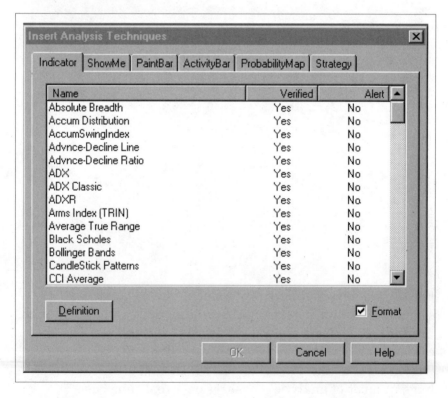

CHAPTER 6 Analytic Indicators and Models

given time. Note, in Figure 6–2, that the cursor is positioned on a point on the RSI line, and an "E" appears on the screen. A trader requesting an expert opinion is provided with an automated interpretation of the indicator, as shown in Figure 6–4. Besides assisting the less-than-expert technician, this feature has the added advantage of being totally objective, as it is generated by using artificial intelligence.

FIGURE 6–4

Automated Expert Analytic Commentary from TradeStation

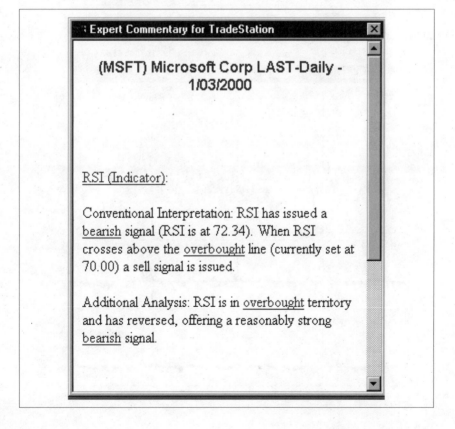

IDENTIFYING TRENDS IN VOLATILITY

Source: BigCharts.com

Price: Free

FIGURE 6-5

Chart of Implied Volatility and Technical Indicators for VIX from BigCharts

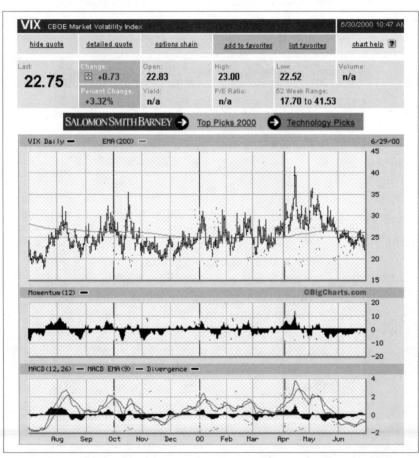

CHAPTER 6 Analytic Indicators and Models 103

FIGURE 6-6

BigCharts Glossary of Analytic Terms

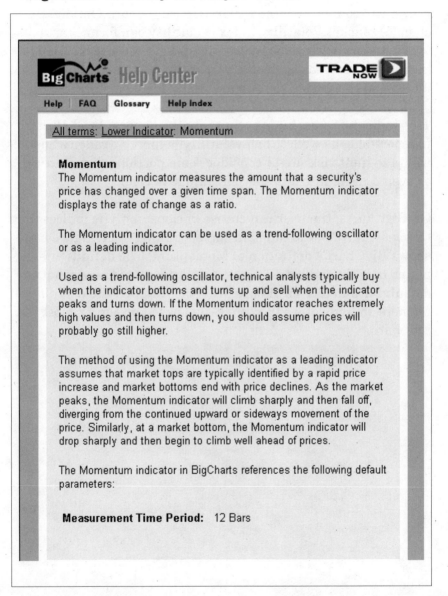

Price isn't the only thing a trader can chart and analyze. As Figure 6–5 shows, one of the indices available for charting on BigCharts.com is VIX: the CBOE (Chicago Board Options Exchange) Market Volatility Index. Volatility can form chart patterns, just as price does. By paying up for a put or call, an options trader increases volatility, just the way the price would increase if the trader paid up for the underlying stock.

This indicator is useful in estimating the general level of risk in a portfolio, as well. When volatility is high, a trader who wants to limit risk might consider some portfolio restucturing, or even a move into a larger percentage of cash.

On BigCharts, the user can choose various analytic indices (in this case, MACD and Momentum) as trading aids. Figure 6–6 shows BigChart's definition of Momentum. The definition explains how the indicator is generally interpreted, and what the default parameters for its use are. For example, the default Momentum indicator of Figure 6–5 is based on the 12 most recent bars.

PART TWO

Fundamental Analysis

Before trading starts in full force each day, most Street trading desks have a short morning meeting, attended by traders, salespeople, and advisory staff such as economists and analysts. The advisors will provide forecasts and commentary on upcoming economic or company events. And the senior traders will describe the activity they saw in their specialized sectors of the market the day before, as well as what activity they anticipate for the upcoming day.

The meeting serves two purposes. It assists each trader to form a coherent opinion from the cacophony of economic and company news transmitted over the computer and squawk box during the trading day. And it serves as a "heads up" to all, ensuring that no trader in the profit center is blindsided by an unknown catalytic event—public or not.

Chapters 7 and 8 describe what kind of news professional traders consider critical, how they dig deep for additional color, and how they anticipate the effect of each upcoming event on market prices.

CHAPTER 7

Economic News and Numbers

In the trading room and on the exchange floor, activity stops before each scheduled release of important economic news. Traders pull their orders and wait for those first few syllables that reveal whether the "number" contains a bullish or bearish surprise. If it does, activity may be so frenzied that the financial futures contracts (such as the bond futures on the CBOT) may trade at two different prices on opposite sides of the pit, forcing exchange officials to declare a "fast market," or one in which brokers are not held to certain executions.

Seconds after release, economists at the larger firms will provide traders and salespeople with a quick-and-dirty instant analysis of the number over the squawk box. The economists will likely follow their first reaction with a more comprehensive analysis of the report a few minutes later, after they have had a chance to digest and interpret all of its details.

U.S. economic news affects every market in the world. Even foreign traders stay up late to watch the important numbers, generally released at 8:30 A.M. EST. But the important numbers have their first and greatest impact on the bond market, where traders profit from gauging the significance of each number on future interest rates.

Changes in interest rates often lead changes in equity prices, if only by a few seconds. Paradoxically, a drop in interest rates caused by evidence of a slowdown in economic growth generally means that the equity markets will rally. Apparently, the benefits to a company that results from lower borrowing costs are more important than the harm caused by a weakening economy.

Exactly which types of economic news are most important can run in cycles. Today, Fed actions and the monthly Employment Report have the biggest impact on the market. But at times in the past, changes in the Commodity Price Index, the exchange rate for dollar/yen, or the Trade Deficit statistics were nearly as important. Individual investors can gauge for themselves the potential of each important economic event by being aware of market expectations for each scheduled event, and then observing market reaction to surprises relative to expectations.

CHAPTER 7   Economic News and Numbers   109

TRACKING THE ECONOMY

Source: Yahoo.com

Price: Free

FIGURE 7-1

Economic Calendar from Yahoo

Economic Calendar								Jul 03 - Jul 07
Last Week								Next Week
Date	Time (ET)	Statistic	For	Actual	Briefing Forecast	Market Expects	Prior	Revised From
Jul 03	12:00 am	Auto Sales	Jun	-	7.0M	6.8M	6.8M	-
	12:00 am	Truck Sales	Jun	-	7.4M	7.4M	7.3M	-
	10:00 am	Construction Spending	May	+0.1%	+0.4%	-0.2%	-1.1%	-0.6%
	10:00 am	NAPM Index	Jun	51.8%	53.0%	53.0%	53.2%	53.2%
Jul 05	10:00 am	Leading Indicators	May	-0.1%	-0.2%	-0.2%	0.0%	-0.1%
	10:00 am	NAPM Services	Jun	-	59.0%	61.5%	61.5%	-
Jul 06	8:30 am	Initial Claims	07/01	296K	308K	305K	308K	306K
	10:00 am	Factory Orders	May	4.1%	3.6%	2.9%	-3.8%	-4.3%
Jul 07	8:30 am	Average Workweek	Jun	-	34.5H	34.5H	34.4H	-
	8:30 am	Hourly Earnings	Jun	-	0.4%	0.4%	0.1%	-
	8:30 am	Nonfarm Payrolls	Jun	-	325K	260K	231K	-
	8:30 am	Unemployment Rate	Jun	-	4.0%	4.0%	4.1%	-

Yahoo.com provides an economic calendar that details past and future news releases whose sources are governmental (for example, unemployment statistics report), academic (for example, the University of Michigan consumer sentiment index), and private (for example, the NAPM, or National Association of Purchasing Managers, report).

Figure 7-1 shows the calendar shortly after release of the monthly employment report on July 7, 2000. In advance of the release, the calendar detailed a forecast from Briefing.com, consensus market expectations (derived from surveys of economists), and the prior month's value for four summary statistics. After the release, it supplied the actual values reported, along with revisions to previous months that were part of the news release.

If the user clicks on the name of the statistic, Yahoo also supplies a short synopsis of the meaning of each report, a rating of the report's importance, and links to additional sites for further detail. Figure 7–2 shows that the unemployment report is rated A, meaning it has a top-ranked ability to move markets.

When the unemployment number is released, most traders give the most weight to the value for *nonfarm payrolls*: a change in the number of Americans employed in full-time, nonfarm jobs. But the actual value of the number is not important; only its deviation from what the market expected. Economists publicize their forecasts for this number for many days before its release, and markets build their consensus into prices. Similarly, a revision to the previous month's values may significantly affect

FIGURE 7–2

Economic Calendar Terms from Yahoo

Economic Calendar Terms　　　　　　　　　　Yahoo! Finance Home

The Employment Report

- Importance (A-F): This release merits an A.
- Source: Bureau of Labor Statistics, U.S. Department of Labor.
- Release Time: First Friday of the month at 8:30 ET for the prior month
- Raw Data Available At: http://stats.bls.gov/news.release/empsit.toc.htm

the market, because it may indicate a change in the trend of the statistic over time.

On July 7 the consensus forecast for nonfarm payrolls was for an increase of 260,000 jobs—historically, quite a significant change. And some economists had forecast even higher values. As the calendar shows, Briefing.com forecast an increase of 325,000 jobs.

But the actual increase was only 11,000 jobs: a major shock to the market. As Figure 5–5 shows, the 30-year bond contract on the CBOT reacted quickly, trading up nearly a full point (lowering yields about 10 basis points) on this indication that the economy was weaker than anticipated. To traders, this implied that the Fed might not need to tighten short-term rates in August.

STUDYING THE DETAIL

Source: BLS.gov

Price: Free

FIGURE 7-3

Employment Situation News Release from BLS

The Employment Situation News Release

Employment Situation Summary

```
Internet address:    http://stats.bls.gov/newsrels.htm
Technical information:              USDL 00-194
   Household data: (202) 691-6378
                                    Transmission of material in this release is
   Establishment data:   691-6555   embargoed until 8:30 A.M. (EDT),
Media contact:           691-5902   Friday, July 7, 2000.

            THE EMPLOYMENT SITUATION: JUNE 2000

   Total nonfarm payroll employment was little changed in June, the Bureau
of Labor Statistics of the U.S. Department of Labor reported today. Private-
sector payroll employment rose by 206,000, following a decline of 165,000
(as revised) in May. The June increase in private payrolls was largely
offset by a decline in federal government employment, as 190,000 temporary
workers hired for the decennial census completed their work. The
unemployment rate was 4.0 percent in June, about the same as in May.
Average hourly earnings increased by 5 cents over the month and by 3.6
percent over the year.
```

A trader who followed the link supplied by Yahoo shown in Figure 7–2 for the employment report would have been directed to the full text of the report supplied by the Bureau of Labor Statistics of the U.S. Department of Labor, available at its own site. Figure 7–3 shows only the first paragraph of the report; the full summary report runs several pages.

CHAPTER 7 Economic News and Numbers

In practice, reports such as this one are supplied to news agencies in advance of their release, but are embargoed until the precise time of release: in this case, 8:30 A.M. EDT on July 7. Because of this procedure, the full text is instantly available to traders over their real-time news services. There have been instances in the past when data was accidentally released early.

As this report shows, God is in the details, and professional traders must consider all the information available to them rather than just the simple summary statistics. For example, as the text of Figure 7–3 shows, the net increase of 11,000 nonfarm jobs (seasonally adjusted) was actually composed of an *increase* of 206,000 jobs in the private sector, which was nearly entirely offset by a *decrease* in federal government employment of 190,000 jobs.

This decrease in federal government employment was caused by the exit from the federal payroll of year 2000 census workers who had completed their work. But it was an event economists could anticipate. Therefore, on close reading, the number did not appear as bullish as the small net increase indicated. This detail may have been responsible for the short-term sell-off in bond futures that followed the initial spike upward, as shown in Figure 5–5.

WATCHING THE FED CALENDAR

Source: FederalReserve.gov

Price: Free

FIGURE 7-4

Federal Reserve Calendar from FederalReserve

AUGUST			
	1	**G.5 Statistical Release** *Foreign Exchange Rates*	**G.13 Statistical Release** *Selected Interest Rates*
	7	**G.19 Statistical Release** *Consumer Credit* 3:00 p.m.	
	9	**Beige Book** 2:00 p.m.	
	15	**G.17 Statistical Release** *Industrial Production and Capacity Utilization* 9:15 a.m.	
	22	**FOMC Meeting**	
	24	**FOMC Minutes** Meeting of June 27-28, 2000 2:00 p.m.	

CHAPTER 7   Economic News and Numbers   115

The Federal Reserve's statisticians also gather some of their own data and release their own numbers, such as the Industrial Production and Capacity Utilization reports. Figure 7–4 shows a typical Fed calendar of events.

Such news releases are important in their own right as an indication of the state of the economy. But more important is the Fed's interpretation of all the data it observes, whether created by the Fed or by another public or private source.

The most important event on the Fed calendar is the FOMC (Federal Open Market Committee) meeting, held about once every six weeks. At the end of this one- or two-day meeting, the FOMC holds a press conference at which it may announce a change in the Fed Funds rate or a change in the Discount rate (the rate charged by the Federal Reserve bank for loans to its member banks). The FOMC can and has taken emergency action between scheduled meetings via a conference call.

Generally, economists anticipate Fed actions, and most of the rate movement precedes the actual news release. But sometimes the result is less certain: The odds may be 50-50 between no action and a tightening of 25 basis points, or 80-20 between a tightening of 25 and 50 basis points.

The FOMC recently started to give the market a little color at the end of each meeting. It might announce no change in rates, for instance, but a bias in favor of tightening, depending on the economic data it has yet to observe. Though the FOMC delays release of the full minutes of its meeting for about a month, the minutes are nevertheless important. The minutes help traders get a feel for the biases of each of the FOMC's nine members, as well as information about future conditions that might trigger Fed action.

WATCHING THE FED

Source: Bloomberg.com

Price: Free

FIGURE 7-5

Fed Watch from Bloomberg

Bloomberg.com provides the trader with a great deal of information designed to assist in anticipating future monetary policy. Figure 7-5 shows Bloomberg's "Fed Watch" page. It includes expert commentary by *Fed watchers* (economists whose specialty is FOMC activity), the text of speeches by Fed governors, and surveys summarizing market expectations for Fed actions.

The FOMC does not want to surprise the markets, because surprised markets are disorderly markets. It would prefer that the market do the Fed's job of tightening or easing rates by anticipating a rate change in baby steps over several weeks. The FOMC seems to keep order and give hints about its future actions via speeches by its members. Therefore, the text of scheduled speeches by its members is closely watched as a predictor of future actions.

FIGURE 7-6

FOMC Announcement Dates from Bloomberg

FOMC Announcement Dates

Historical Change in Monetary Policy
2000 Meetings

Announcement	Rate	Bias	Time
Start of 2000	5.50%	Neutral	****
Feb 02, 2000	5.75%	Inflation	2:15
Mar 21, 2000	6.00%	Inflation	2:15
May 16, 2000	6.50%	Inflation	2:15
June 28, 2000	—	—	—
Aug 22, 2000	—	—	—
Oct 03, 2000	—	—	—
Nov 15, 2000	—	—	—
Dec 19, 2000	—	—	—

The historical summary of past actions—as well as the bias the Fed has been indicating after each FOMC meeting—is summarized in the report of Figure 7–6. Note that three out of four times in 2000 to date, the Fed's bias was a reliable indicator of the Fed move. This history also shows that the Fed prefers to act gradually, reassessing the effect of each of its actions on the economy. It preferred to make three moves totaling 100 basis points instead of one move of 100 basis points. Because interest rates are of paramount importance to all markets, such a systematic pattern over time tends to create trends in all types of securities.

CHAPTER 7   Economic News and Numbers   119

GETTING REAL-TIME ECONOMIC NEWS

Source: Bloomberg.com

Price: Free

FIGURE 7-7

Market Monitor from Bloomberg

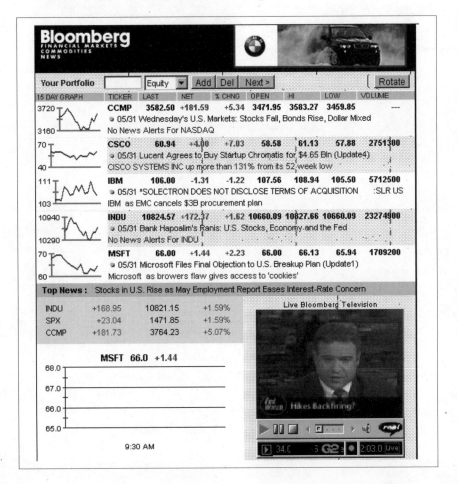

One of the fastest ways for an individual investor to get information about an economic news release is to watch it on television. Bloomberg.com's Market Monitor allows users with sufficiently fast Internet connections to watch live Bloomberg Television on their computer. As Figure 7–7 shows, Market Monitor resides in a window that a trader can keep open on the computer while performing other activities. It also displays news and delayed prices for the trader's choice of securities and the major indices.

CHAPTER 8

Corporate Actions, News, and Rumors

When an institutional salesperson attempts to sell a client on the idea of buying what is touted as an underpriced stock, the client is likely to ask, "What's the catalyst?" In other words, the client wants to know what event is imminent that will cause other investors to recognize the security's value and pay up for it until it reaches a lofty target price.

A report on the state of the economy can serve as a catalyst. So can company announcements, news, and filings with the SEC. But individuals can serve as catalysts, too. If a well-respected portfolio manager or analyst appears on CNBC touting a stock, the price will likely react instantly.

Institutional investors recognize that the price of a security rarely trends monotonically toward true value, but reaches that price in fits and starts that are often triggered by a series of catalysts. Investors prefer immediate gratification when they buy a stock; otherwise, they are exposed to market risk from unexpected sources while they wait.

The diligent trader needs to be aware of every scheduled event on the horizon as a potential market mover, as well as the market's expectations for events such as earnings reports or merger votes. And a trader who is familiar with the company's business and its plans for the future is more likely to estimate the impact of qualitative news on price both quickly and accurately.

CHAPTER 8   Corporate Actions, News, and Rumors   123

WATCHING THE EARNINGS CALENDAR

Source: MSN.com

Price: Free

FIGURE 8-1

Earnings Calendar from MSN

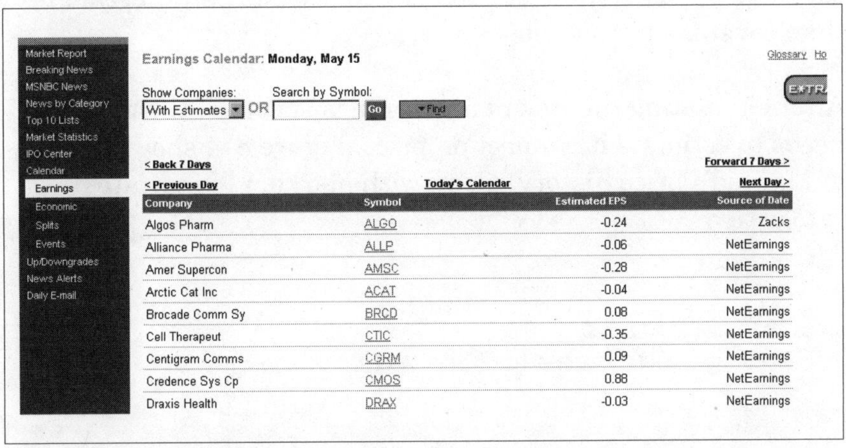

Company	Symbol	Estimated EPS	Source of Date
Algos Pharm	ALGO	-0.24	Zacks
Alliance Pharma	ALLP	-0.06	NetEarnings
Amer Supercon	AMSC	-0.28	NetEarnings
Arctic Cat Inc	ACAT	-0.04	NetEarnings
Brocade Comm Sy	BRCD	0.08	NetEarnings
Cell Therapeut	CTIC	-0.35	NetEarnings
Centigram Comms	CGRM	0.09	NetEarnings
Credence Sys Cp	CMOS	0.88	NetEarnings
Draxis Health	DRAX	-0.03	NetEarnings

One of the most important catalysts for price change is the earnings report. As shown in Figure 8-1, MSN.com provides a handy heads up with expected announcement dates and credible estimates of *EPS* (earnings per share).

Like economic statistics, the value of EPS matters far less than its difference from estimates. But the earnings of some companies are more predictable than others. MSN also allows the trader to gauge the probability of an earnings surprise in two ways.

First, a trader can compare past estimates to actual results. Figure 8–2 shows that the actual earnings of Limited, Inc. can sometimes deviate significantly from the estimates.

Second, the trader can examine the *range* of earnings estimates. As a comparison of Figures 8–2 and 8–3 shows, the number is more likely to be on target if there is less deviance between the high and low estimates for all analysts. Likewise, coverage by many analysts is likely to provide better estimates than coverage by just one or two.

After estimating the risk of an earnings surprise, the trader needs to estimate its impact on price. Figure 8–4 shows a chart of Limited's price history, along with markers to indicate corporate actions.

FIGURE 8–2

Earnings Surprises for Limited, Inc. from MSN

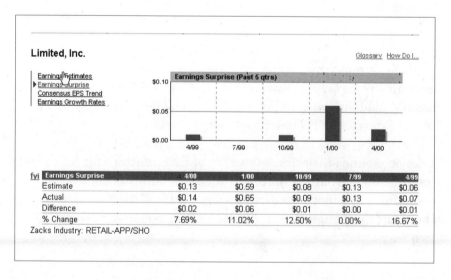

Earnings Surprise	4/00	1/00	10/99	7/99	4/99
Estimate	$0.13	$0.59	$0.08	$0.13	$0.06
Actual	$0.14	$0.65	$0.09	$0.13	$0.07
Difference	$0.02	$0.06	$0.01	$0.00	$0.01
% Change	7.69%	11.02%	12.50%	0.00%	16.67%

Zacks Industry: RETAIL-APP/SHO

CHAPTER 8 Corporate Actions, News, and Rumors

FIGURE 8-3

Earnings Estimates for Limited, Inc. from MSN

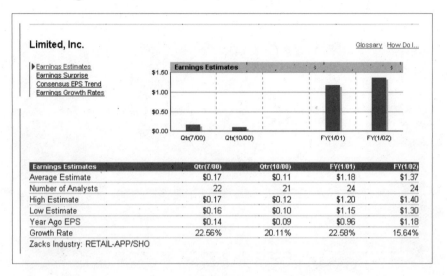

There are two types shown: Markers with "D" indicate dividends or other distributions, and markers with a diagonal flag indicate a stock split. As shown on this chart, if the user puts the cursor on one of the markers, details of the events are shown in a pop-up box, as with the stock split of May 31. Note that when a stock split occurs, all charting services adjust the historical prices to account for the split, so there is no discontinuity in the chart.

Because corporate actions are recorded on their effective date rather than their announcement date, the user must sometimes examine the price action a few days earlier to estimate the impact of the announcement. For example, the dividend denoted March 1 was announced on February 22. But by zooming in on the chart near that date, the user can determine that Limited closed up 13/32 on Feb 22.

FIGURE 8-4

Price History with Corporate Actions for Limited, Inc. from MSN

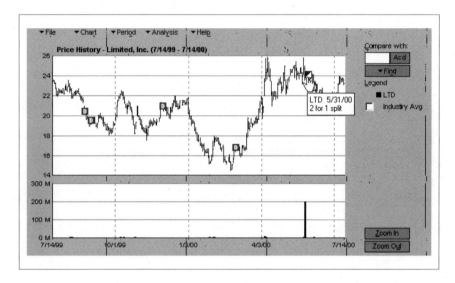

CHAPTER 8 Corporate Actions, News, and Rumors

REAL-TIME ALERTS OF NEWS AND RUMORS

Source: TheFlyOnTheWall.com

Price: Premium

FIGURE 8-5
News Alerts for All Securities from TheFlyOnTheWall

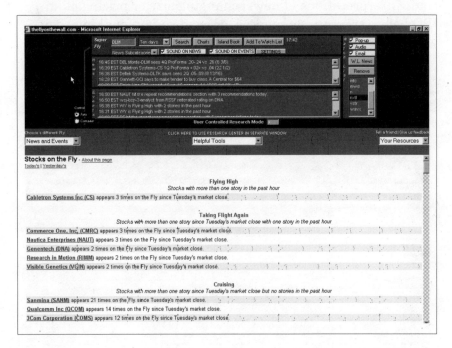

TheFlyOnTheWall.com provides unique real-time alerts. Figure 8-5 illustrates its Stocks on the Flyfeature, in which the system counts the number of recent news alerts in one of three categories, in order of declining urgency: Flying High, which includes stocks with more than one story in the past hour;

Taking Flight Again, which includes stocks with more than one story since the previous close and one story in the last hour; and Cruising, which includes stocks with more than one story since the previous close and no stories in the last hour.

What sets TheFlyOnTheWall apart from other news services is its contributors. Rather than reiterate stories from the major news wires, TheFlyOnTheWall receives its information from professional traders and fund managers. So its alerts may include interpretations of news, changing size or pricing of an IPO before trading commences, or even rumors making their way through the marketplace.

FIGURE 8-6

Site Cross Reference for Exodus Communications from TheFlyOnTheWall

CHAPTER 8 Corporate Actions, News, and Rumors

TheFlyOnTheWall also allows the trader to create a watch list of ten securities. When a new item hits the tape, the system will alert the trader by sound, a pop-up box, or email.

Or an investor can view the stories for just one security, as is shown in Figure 8–6. The Site Cross Reference page shows recent news, rumors, and recommendations for Exodus Communications on July 17, 2000. It also provides the trader with a heads up on upcoming events of significance, such as a company meeting scheduled for a few days hence.

Since the most recent news item relates a rumor about an acquisition, such a meeting—at which material events might be revealed—could trigger a large price move. Note that Figure 8–7 shows the price of Exodus rallied that day, but most of its price appreciation came well after the 8:20 A.M. EST story.

FIGURE 8-7

Daily Price Chart for Exodus Communications from TheFlyOnTheWall

CHAPTER 8 Corporate Actions, News, and Rumors

RESEARCHING COMPANY FILINGS

Source: Edgar-Online.com

Price: Free and Premium

FIGURE 8-8
Recent Filings for Sprint, Inc. from Edgar-Online

Every public company in the United States is required by the SEC to file documents revealing key business and financial information. Edgar-Online.com allows the user access to these filings. The filings contain factual material about the company and its plans, as well as commentary and warnings about its future business prospects.

The Edgar report of Figure 8–8 references the 8-K report of October 6, 1999, a "Report of Unscheduled Material Events" for Sprint Corp.

On October 4, 1999, MCI WorldCom and Sprint announced a definitive merger agreement whereby MCI WorldCom would acquire Sprint for $115 million in stock, topping a rival proposal by BellSouth. However, the headline was just the sound bite; the details of the acquisition were more complex and uncertain.

A careful reading of the actual filing (a document well over 100 pages long) revealed the primary obstacles to the merger. First, the company warned that "the merger is subject to the approvals of Sprint and MCI WorldCom shareholders as well as approvals from the FCC, the Justice Department, various state government bodies and foreign antitrust authorities." The filing also indicated that the approval process would take many months: WorldCom expected the merger to be consummated in the second half of 2000.

These were not just boilerplate caveats; given the size of the two entities, there was a real possibility that regulators both in the United States and in Europe might quash the merger based on antitrust concerns. The anticipated nine-plus months to completion were another indication of the degree of difficulty of regulatory approval.

CHAPTER 8 Corporate Actions, News, and Rumors   133

When the merger was announced, some traders took positions based on the value of the new enterprise. But *arbitrageurs* (traders who profit on small inefficiencies between securities) quickly focused on the mechanics of the acquisition buried deep in the text. Based on the relative prices of all the securities involved, the estimated probabilities of regulatory and shareholder approval, and the anticipated length of time until resolution one way or another, an arbitrageur could model the merger and set large and complex positions from which that arbitrageur could expect to profit.

Under the agreement, each share of Sprint PCS stock would be exchanged for $76 of MCI WorldCom common stock, subject to a *collar* (a range above and below current market prices outside of which the deal would not be done). In addition, each share of Sprint PCS stock would be exchanged for one share of a new WorldCom PCS tracking stock and 0.116025 shares of MCI WorldCom common stock.

That is, a trader who bought one share of Sprint would receive $76 of WorldCom stock assuming that the deal went through. At the time of the announcement, the trader did not know how many shares of WorldCom stock $76 would buy. Conversely, a trader who bought one share of Sprint PCS would receive one share of a new WorldCom PCS tracking stock and 0.116025 shares of MCI WorldCom stock if the deal went through.

This summary doesn't begin to describe the level of mathematical complexity in the merger. Often, the rules were structured to prevent price manipulation by arbitrageurs. Not until page 58 of the filing document was it revealed how average price (one of the terms in the equation) was calculated:

(n) "Average Price" means the average (rounded to the nearest 1/10,000) of the volume weighted averages (rounded to the nearest 1/10,000) of the trading prices of MCI WorldCom Common Stock on The Nasdaq National Market ("Nasdaq"), as reported by Bloomberg Financial Markets (or such other source as the parties shall agree in writing), for the 15 trading days randomly selected by lot by MCI WorldCom and Sprint together from the 30 consecutive trading days ending on the third trading day immediately preceding the Effective Time.

All the securities involved in the merger were mathematically linked as long as the merger appeared probable. If one security became expensive relative to the others, an arbitrageur would sell that security and buy the others in carefully calculated ratios.

On November 13 and 14, 1999, the Justice Department and the FCC issued separate warnings that they would look closely at the deal. On February 21, 2000, the European Commission warned that it would require four months to review the anticipated impact of the merger.

During the months following the initial filing, MCI WorldCom engaged in a lobbying effort to convince both regulators and institutional investors that the merger would have a positive impact on both consumer services and the competitive environment. It failed to do so: On May 17, 2000, U.S. regulators recommended that the deal be blocked. On June 22, 2000 (four months and one day after the start of the European Commission's four-month review process), WorldCom officials responded with a counteroffer: WorldCom would sell off $45 to $50 billion worth of Sprint's assets, including its long distance business and its Internet services, to a third party.

This offer was a case of too little, too late. The commission said that it blocked the merger because it "would have resulted in

CHAPTER 8 Corporate Actions, News, and Rumors

FIGURE 8-9

Price Chart of WorldCom, Inc. versus Sprint Corp. from MSN

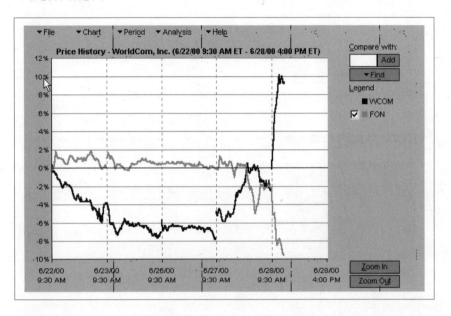

the creation of a dominant position in the market for top-level universal Internet connectivity." And, the last minute offer to divest itself of part of its assets was deemed "insufficient to resolve the competition concerns resulting from the merger."

Figure 8–9 shows the results of the blocked merger. The prices of WorldCom and Sprint became disengaged, and liquidation of arbitrage positions assisted in causing spikes in the price of each security.

EVALUATING IPOS

Source: IPO.com

Price: Free

FIGURE 8-10
IPO.com Index for July 19, 2000, from IPO

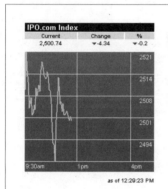

IPO.com offers investors the ability to evaluate companies just before and after they have completed an *IPO* (Initial Public Offering). The site includes basic fundamental information about the company and its outlook, offering information, and calendars of important dates.

IPO.com also tracks IPOs beyond their first trading date. Figure 8–10 shows an intraday chart of its IPO.com Index, an index calculated from the ratio of the current market price to initial offering price and multiplied by 100 for the 100 most recently issued IPOs. On the date of the chart, the index included IPOs from the previous three months. Its current price of $2500.74 meant that on average, IPOs issued within the past three months had appreciated 150 percent: better than a 600 percent increase if annualized.

This appreciation does not necessarily mean that IPOs are always a good buy. An underwriter first offers participation in a hot IPO to its best institutional clients, at an offering price that allegedly ensures that all of the stock is sold. And for a really hot IPO, even the best clients may be allocated only a small percentage of what they are willing to buy.

An individual investor would not be able to buy the stock of such an IPO until it started to trade in the open market, and that price is often substantially higher than the final price of the IPO.

FIGURE 8–11

Offering Information for Support.com on July 19, 2000, from IPO

SUPPORT.COM INC.

Company Info | Offering Info | News & Events | Aftermarket

Offering Status	
Current IPO Status:	Priced
Symbol:	SPRT
Exchange:	NASDAQ
Form Filed:	S-1
Share Type:	Common Stock
Final Offering Amount:	$59,500,000
Final Price:	$14.00
Est. Offering Expenses:	$1,200,000
Total Shares:	4,250,000

Key Dates	
Filing Date:	2/18/00
Pricing Date:	7/18/00

Underwriters

Role	Name
Lead Manager	Credit Suisse First Boston
Co-Manager	Chase H&Q
Co-Manager	Bear, Stearns & Co. Inc.
Co-Manager	Wit Soundview

Figure 8–11 shows offering information for Support.com, Inc., an IPO that commenced trading on July 19, 2000. The user can also link to background information on the company, news and events, and details of aftermarket trading.

IPO.com also provides schedules showing when recent IPOs will leave their *quiet period* (a period 40 or 90 days long, during which the issuer is not allowed to publicize the stock) and their *lockup period* (a period up to 180 days long during which outsiders are prohibited from selling their stock).

These dates are important to an investor because they indicate the possibility of catalysts important to the price of the stock. Publicity after the quiet period may generate bullish triggers, such as an analyst's buy recommendation. Or insider selling after the lockup period may generate bearish triggers, such as sizable insider selling by officers wishing to cash out.

CHAPTER 8 Corporate Actions, News, and Rumors

LISTENING TO INSIDER TALK ON IPOs

Source: TheFlyOnTheWall.com

Price: Premium

FIGURE 8-12

IPO "Deals in Demand" Report for July 17, 2000, from TheFlyOnTheWall

In addition to the real-time information it provides about the secondary market, TheFlyOnTheWall.com provides real-time commentary on IPOs from institutional investors. Figure 8–12

FIGURE 8-13

Detail about Blue Martini Software from TheFlyOnTheWall

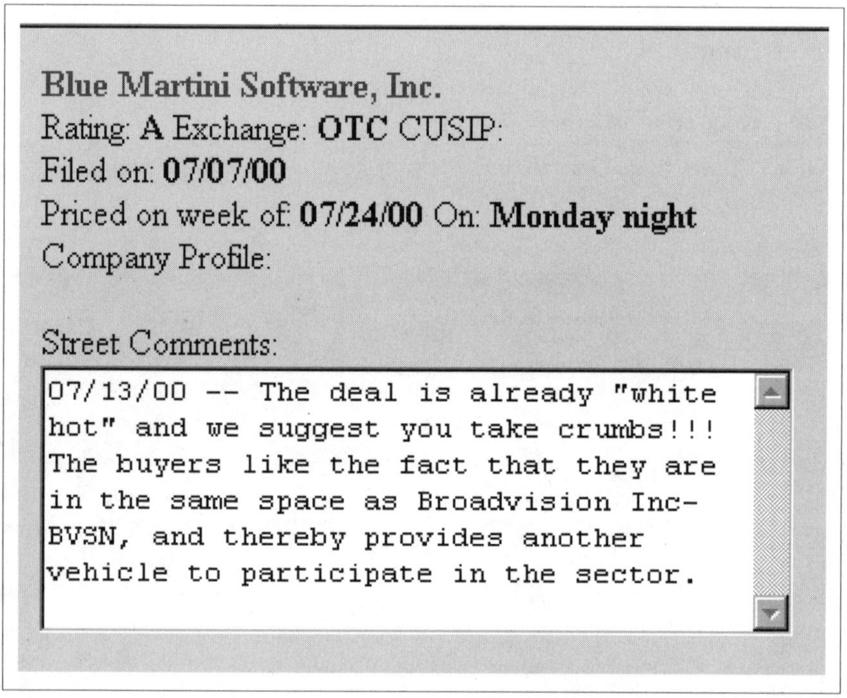

Blue Martini Software, Inc.
Rating: A Exchange: **OTC** CUSIP:
Filed on: **07/07/00**
Priced on week of: **07/24/00** On: **Monday night**
Company Profile:

Street Comments:

```
07/13/00 -- The deal is already "white
hot" and we suggest you take crumbs!!!
The buyers like the fact that they are
in the same space as Broadvision Inc-
BVSN, and thereby provides another
vehicle to participate in the sector.
```

---

shows its Deals in Demand page, which details current size and pricing estimates for deals considered hot.

As Figure 8–13 shows, the user can click on the Details button to obtain ad hoc Street comments unlikely to hit the news wires. When these comments relate only the author's opinion, they must be taken with a grain of salt, since the author's name and affiliation are not revealed. However, comments that

FIGURE 8-14

News and Events for Support, Inc. on July 19, 2000, from TheFlyOnTheWall

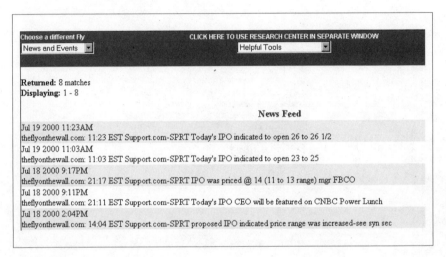

relate fact (such as those shown in Figure 8–14) are more objective.

Note the progress of the Support.com IPO on July 19, its first day of trading. Although the pricing estimate two days earlier had been $8 to $10 per share, the deal was priced on the evening of July 18 at $14. By 11:03 A.M. traders estimated that Support.com would open at $23 to $25, finally indicating an open of $26 to $26 1/2 at 11:23 A.M.

As the chart of Figure 8–15 shows, this indication was accurate. Shortly after trading commenced, Support.com's stock shot up to $39 3/16, a half-hour gain of 180 percent for those who paid $14. An individual investor, on the other hand, probably couldn't have bought stock for less than $30.

FIGURE 8-15

Chart of Support, Inc. on July 19, 2000, from TheFlyOnTheWall

KEEPING UP WITH THE NEWS

Source: Validea.com

Price: Free

FIGURE 8-16

New Ideas in Technology from Validea

Symbol	Company Name	Price (Prev. Day Close)	Source	Date	Action
SLR	SOLECTRON CORP	$47.38	CNBC	7/19/00	Reporting
NTAP	NETWORK APPLIANCE INC	$112.56	CNBC	7/14/00	Reporting
CMRC	COMMERCE ONE INC	$57.44	TheStreet.com	7/12/00	Reporting
SDLI	SDL INC	$428.06	CNNfn (Online)	7/7/00	Reporting
GLW	CORNING INC	$275.63	CNNfn (Online)	7/7/00	Reporting
LU	LUCENT TECHNOLOGIES INC	$54.25	CNNfn (Online)	7/6/00	Reporting
INTC	INTEL CORP	$142.69	CNNfn (Online)	7/6/00	Reporting
NOK	NOKIA CORP ADS	$54.50	CNNfn (Online)	7/6/00	Reporting
CSCO	CISCO SYSTEMS INC	$69.50	CNNfn (Online)	7/6/00	Reporting
ENT	EQUANT NV	$41.00	WorldlyInvestor	7/5/00	Pick
TMWD	TUMBLEWEED COMMUNICATION	$65.06	CNBC (TV)	7/1/00	Reporting
USIX	USINTERNETWORKING INC	$21.06	CNNfn (Online)	6/29/00	Reporting
CRA	PE CORP CELERA GENOMICS	$110.00	CNNfn (Online)	6/29/00	Reporting
CPQ	COMPAQ COMPUTER CORP	$27.81	CNNfn (Online)	6/29/00	Reporting
EFNT	EFFICIENT NETWORKS INC	$90.86	CNBC.com	6/28/00	Reporting

Validea.com allows the user to find recent references to a stock or sector, and rank the results by the number of occurrences. It also ranks the quality of the sources and analysts in various ways. As Figure 8–16 shows, the user can limit the search to impeccable sources (the minimum source rating is set to five stars). The stories come from print, television, and on-line media sources.

One would expect a high number of stories about stocks such as Intel, Nokia, and Cisco. But the number one rank of Solectron Corp. (SLR) is worthy of attention.

FIGURE 8–17

Buzz Report for Solectron Corp. from Validea

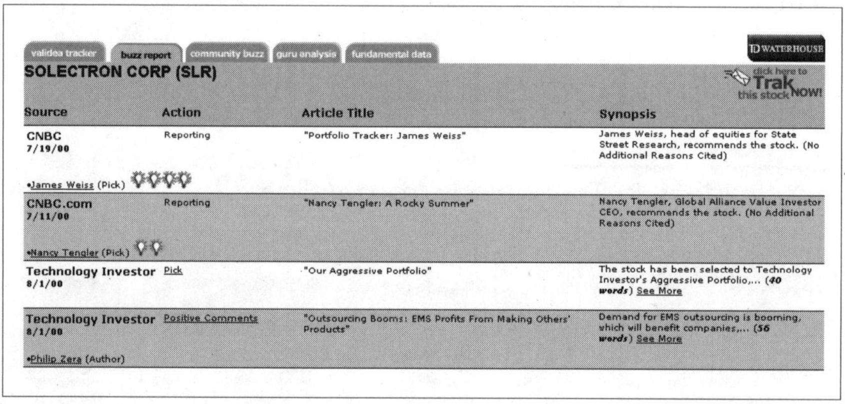

validea tracker | buzz report | community buzz | guru analysis | fundamental data

TD WATERHOUSE

SOLECTRON CORP (SLR)

click here to Trak this stock NOW!

Source	Action	Article Title	Synopsis
CNBC 7/19/00 •James Weiss (Pick)	Reporting	"Portfolio Tracker: James Weiss"	James Weiss, head of equities for State Street Research, recommends the stock. (No Additional Reasons Cited)
CNBC.com 7/11/00 •Nancy Tengler (Pick)	Reporting	"Nancy Tengler: A Rocky Summer"	Nancy Tengler, Global Alliance Value Investor CEO, recommends the stock. (No Additional Reasons Cited)
Technology Investor 8/1/00	Pick	"Our Aggressive Portfolio"	The stock has been selected to Technology Investor's Aggressive Portfolio,... (*40 words*) See More
Technology Investor 8/1/00 •Philip Zera (Author)	Positive Comments	"Outsourcing Booms: EMS Profits From Making Others' Products"	Demand for EMS outsourcing is booming, which will benefit companies,... (*56 words*) See More

Validea also provides a Buzz Report that summarizes recent stories about a stock. As Figure 8–17 shows, Solectron has received quite a bit of media attention, all favorable. However, an investor must be careful about using this information.

As favorable as the fundamentals might be, the technicals may be another story. It is possible that anyone who might be motivated to buy the stock by such stories has already done so. Further, institutional owners of a stock generally recommend it only after they've finished buying their position. So it's reasonable for a buyer who likes Solectron's fundamentals to analyze its technicals as well. The wisest course of action may be to wait for a buying opportunity.

CHAPTER 8 Corporate Actions, News, and Rumors

LINKS TO NEWS SOURCES

Source: JustQuotes.com

Price: Free

FIGURE 8-18

News and Analyst Links for Exodus Communications from JustQuotes

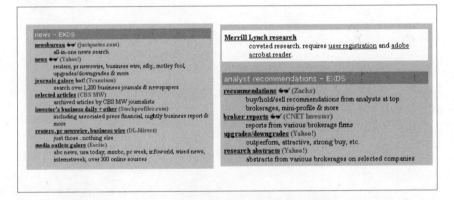

JustQuotes provides links to Internet resources on a company basis. As Figure 8–18 shows, the user can search a variety of media sources for information about a specific stock (in this case, Exodus Communications) and link to research and recommendations about that stock.

In addition to links for news and analyst recommendations, JustQuotes also provides links to information about company profiles, insider activity, returns, competitors, corporate actions, historical prices, charts, earnings, financial statements, SEC filings, financial ratios, and discussion forums.

PART THREE
Trade Selection

Ideally, a professional investor wants to be the first one though the doorway: The investor hopes to identify the next Microsoft and buy it before anyone else catches on. To aid in the search for new ideas, the professional investor can access both analytic tools and expert advice.

When initiating a search, a portfolio manager may start with constraints that restrict its scope. For example, the manager may want to be heavily invested in the wireless communications sector and to find the best securities within that sector. Or the manager may want to remain open to the entire universe of potential investments.

The following three chapters describe how professionals use analytic tools to retrieve historical data, and filter and rank that data according to rules that they specify, leaving them with a short list of investment candidates or trading strategies they can investigate in depth. These chapters also describe how professionals use expert advice, and how they vet the source and reliability of that advice.

CHAPTER 9

Fundamental Screening, Back Testing, and Securities Selection

Including both foreign and domestic instruments of all asset types, there are over 45,000 different securities from which to choose when searching for a trade. To make that search manageable, institutional investors use quantitative tools to filter and rank all securities by their choice of fundamental characteristics.

Some of these fundamental characteristics are backward looking: Figures and ratios involving past revenue, earnings, and book value are old news. Nonetheless, an investor or analyst can use such statistics to filter out from consideration companies that do not meet minimum standards for growth, profitability, or financial health.

Other characteristics are forward looking: Consensus analysts' opinions and projections for EPS growth are only forecasts. But when combined with historic statistics, the backward- and forward-looking characteristics can identify securities with an intriguing pattern of growth.

Although the Internet offers expert analysts the ability to perform sophisticated analyses of their own design, it also offers expert aid to amateurs. Several sites provide preprogrammed screens designed to identify securities likely to appreciate in the future.

Individual investors must keep in mind that the purpose of fundamental screens is to identify value, and value is not always reflected in market price. Professional investors know that the market is composed of humans, and that human estimates of value may sometimes be less than rational. They also understand that investors have many reasons for buying or failing to buy a security—some rational, some not. Professionals would never contend that the market is wrong when, in their opinion, other investors have failed to recognize the value of the professionals' favorite holdings. Chat room conversations show that only amateurs blame the marketplace rather than themselves for their losses.

Still, a stock that is undervalued can be expected to appreciate over time. And by considering technical indicators and trigger events when optimizing the timing of entry into a position, an investor reduces short-term market risk. Then, the investor can wait for the world to agree with the estimate of value.

CHAPTER 9 Fundamental Screening, Back Testing, and Securities Selection   151

SCREENING FOR TRADE IDEAS

Source: MSN.com

Price: Free

FIGURE 9-1

Stock Finder Custom Screen from MSN

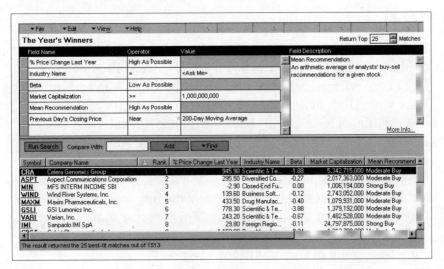

MSN.com offers Finder, a powerful analytic tool that allows the user to screen for and rank securities that meet fundamental and technical criteria.

The type of data on which the user can base the search includes Company Basics (for example, Industry Name), Price Ratios (for example, Price/Sales Ratio), Trading and Volume (for example, Percent Institutional Ownership, Beta), Stock Price History (for example, 52-Week High), Analyst Projections (for example, Mean Recommendation), and Advisor FYI (for example, Price Up in Heavy Volume).

MSN also offers several preprogrammed searches, both straightforward (for example, Small-Cap Stocks with High Momentum) and exotic (for example, Contrarian Strategy). The user could also start with one of these stock searches and add or modify its rules. Also, the search rules can be saved for future use.

Figure 9–1 shows a stock screen run of June 30, 2000, intended to identify large-cap stocks (Market Capitalization >= 1 billion) with significant price appreciation (% Price Change Last Year High as Possible) but with low volatility (Beta[1] Low as Possible). These are all backward-looking statistics, so one forward- looking statistic is included as well: Analysts must view the stock favorably (Mean Recommendation as High as Possible). And finally, the price of the stock must be near a technical support level—the 200-day moving average (Previous Day's Closing Price Near 200-day Moving Average).

Note that some of the conditions are precise (for example, Market Capitalization >= 1,000,000,000) while others are fuzzy (Beta Low as Possible). Finder ranks all stocks that meet the discrete criteria in order of how well they meet the fuzzy criteria. The program can be set up to query the user for the value of a parameter (for example, Industry Name = <Ask Me). Finder also allows the user to create an equation that's a function of one or more of the stored variables.

---

[1] Beta is a measure of the relative volatility of the stock.

CHAPTER 9   Fundamental Screening, Back Testing, and Securities Selection   **153**

As the report shows, Celera Genomics ranked number one when all industry groups were allowed. Figure 9–2 shows a chart of Celera Genomics on the date of the screen, along with select technical indicators. The chart shows why it ranked high in the search: As Finder's results show, the price of Celera Genomics appreciated 945 percent during 1999, and its current price is just above its 200-day moving average. But the stock is also volatile, having rallied up about 100 points and back down about 50, all in the course of a month or so. Although the model requested a stock with a Beta as low as possible, Celera Genomics' excellent fit of the other criteria outweighed this single failure. Nonetheless, its Beta might disqualify it from consideration by a risk-averse investor.

FIGURE 9–2

Chart of Celera Genomics with Technical Indicators from MSN

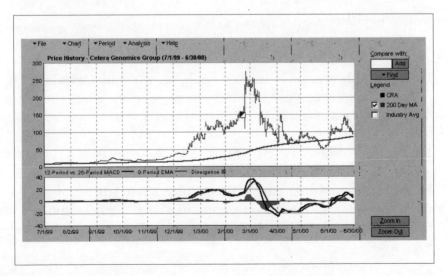

BACK-TESTING FUNDAMENTAL CRITERIA

Source: MSN.com

Price: Free

FIGURE 9-3

Stock Finder Search for Low P/E from MSN

Symbol	Company Name	Rank	% Price Change Last Year	Industry Name	P/E Ratio: 1 Ye...
MTLX	Marine Transport Corporation	1	-27.60	Shipping	0.50
FILM	INTELEFILM Corp.	2	14.40	Broadcasting -...	0.60
BIME	Biomune Systems, Inc.	3	-47.10	Diagnostic Su...	0.70
CXSN	Counsel Corporation	4	-19.30	Diversified Inv...	0.70
NEW...	New England Realty Associates Limit...	5	36.40	Property Mana...	0.80
AMS	American Shared Hospital Services	6	4.70	Specialized H...	0.90
RAY	Raytech Corporation	7	-25.00	Industrial Equi...	0.90
ATEA	Astea International Inc.	8	-59.70	Application So...	1.00
FLYA	CHC Helicopter Corporation	9	10.50	Air Services, O...	1.30
IMCI	Infinite Group, Inc.	10	50.60	Industrial Elect...	1.30

Because MSN.com includes in its data set some historical information, the user can use its Finder feature to back-test the predictive abilities of some common statistics.

For example, Figures 9–3 and 9–4 show the results of a custom screen that finds the top ten and bottom ten stocks as ranked by P/E ratios one year ago. Theoretically, those with a low P/E might have represented value, and have been a buy, while those with a high P/E might have been overbought, and have been a sell.

FIGURE 9-4

Stock Finder Search for High P/E from MSN

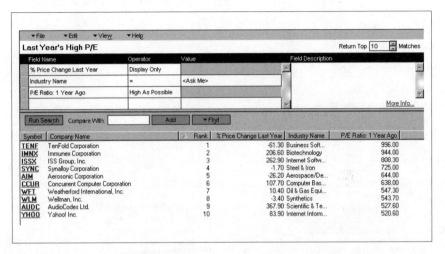

Instead, the return of many of the *low* P/E stocks was poor: Half of them lost money over the last year, while two lost about 50 percent of their value. Conversely, the return of many of the *high* P/E stocks was good: Three gained over 200 percent of their value. These results indicate that there is often a very good reason why a stock is trading where it is. A wary investor needs to find the story behind the statistics.

USING PREDEFINED SEARCHES BASED ON FUNDAMENTAL DATA

Source: WallStreetCity.com

Price: Free and Premium

FIGURE 9-5

Predefined Fundamental Searches from WallStreetCity

Stories | Searches

Stocks with Reversal Potential
- Projected Growth Stocks
- High Projected Growth
- Intermediate Term
- Long Term
- High Earnings Growth 1

Strong Stocks
- High Volume w/EarningsUpgrades
- Strong w/ Good Fundamentals
- Strongest in the Last 6 Wks
- Strong in Multiple Time Periods
- Weak Stocks / Recently Strong

Overvalued Stocks
- by High Price/Sales Ratio
- by High Price/Book Value Ratio
- Unattractive Fundamentals/Tech.
- Unattractive Fundamentals/Perf.

Insider, Institutions & Short Interest
- High Insider Buying
- Surging Insider Trading
- High Short Interest Ratio
- Owned by the Fewest Institutions

Stories | Searches

Searching Using Earnings Criteria
- Lowest Price Earnings Ratio
- High Earnings Velocity
- Price Earnings Ratio
- Low Projected Earnings
- Positive Revision in Projected EPS
- Earnings Stability, + Value Ranks
- Attractive Gross Margin
- Great EPS, Sales, Cash Flow
- High Sales Growth, Strong ROS
- Very + Sales/Cash Flow Ratios

Weak Stocks
- Strong Stocks / Recently Weak
- Weakest in the Last 3 Weeks
- Weakest in the Last 6 Weeks
- Weak Stocks Recovering

Undervalued Stocks
- Stocks
- Growth Stock Strategy 1
- Growth Stock Strategy 2
- by Price/X Ratio
- by Low Price Book Ratio

Cash Flow
- Exc. Cash Flow Growth
- Exc. Free C.F./Share, Good Growth

CHAPTER 9 Fundamental Screening, Back Testing, and Securities Selection   157

FIGURE 9-6

Projected Growth Stocks with Reverse Potential from WallStreetCity

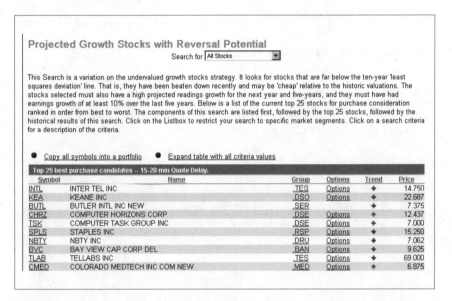

As Figure 9–5 shows, WallStreetCity.com has created a diverse set of predefined screens tested by its in-house analysts and intended to identify stocks that represent value, as well as stocks with a bullish or bearish trading pattern.

For example, Figure 9–6 shows the results of a search for stocks that have been beaten down and may now be poised for recovery. Note that when a screen is run, the report includes a description of the rules applied and the logic behind them.

VIEWING GRAPHIC REPRESENTATIONS OF VALUE

Source: MorningStar.com

Price: Free and Premium

FIGURE 9-7

Predefined Fundamental Searches as of July 21, 2000, from WallStreetCity

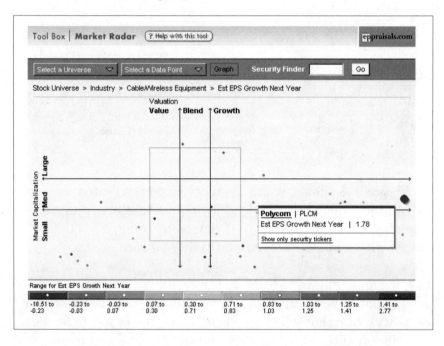

Morningstar.com provides the investor with Market Radar, a graphic tool for stock selection. As shown in Figure 9–7, Morningstar creates a scatter plot of all stocks within a universe specified by the user, in this case, Cable and Wireless

CHAPTER 9 Fundamental Screening, Back Testing, and Securities Selection   159

Equipment. The vertical axis is market capitalization, broken into small-, medium-, and large-cap regions. The horizontal axis is valuation characteristics, broken into value, blend, and growth regions. Morningstar determines the value of a stock by its own algorithms based on the price/earnings ratio and the price/book ratios of the stock.

Each point plotted on the graph is color-coded to indicate its desirability based on a user-specified parameter: in this case, Estimated EPS Growth Next Year. As the colored bins (shown here as various shades of gray) at the bottom of the graph show, each color indicates a range of values for this parameter. The bin with the highest value is the rightmost; in color, it's dark green. So an investor who is searching for a medium- or large-cap growth company with high estimated EPS growth can click on dark green points in the appropriate grids, and a pop-up box will identify the stock.

As the Market Radar chart shows, one such security is Polycom Inc. Just two days earlier Polycom had reported that second quarter revenues had increased 69 percent, which may have caused analysts to revise upward their estimates for EPS growth.

Of course, market cap, valuation, and EPS estimates are insufficient information on which to base an investment decision. Figure 9–8 shows a portion of Morningstar's "M*Stock Grades" analysis, which grades a security on criteria such as growth, profitability, financial health, and valuation.

FIGURE 9-8

M*Stock Grades for Polycom from WallStreetCity

Morningstar Quicktake® Report | M* Stock Grades   Add PLCM to My Portfolio

Polycom PLCM   **JPMorgan**

Growth Grade: A   What is this?
Fiscal year-end: December

	1996	1997	1998	1999
Sales %	55.6	29.2	131.9	71.2
Earnings/Share %	NMF	NMF	NMF	76.1
Book Value/Share %	---	NMF	26.1	96.6
Dividends/Share %	NMF	NMF	NMF	NMF

View company's forecasted earnings growth

Profitability Grade: C+   What is this?
Fiscal year-end: December   TTM = Trailing 12 Months

	1995	1996	1997	1998	1999	TTM
Return on Assets %	-9.1	3.6	-31.7	19.9	17.8	17.0
Industry Rank	77	39	82	2	5	7
Return on Equity %	NMF	4.3	-52.3	28.9	25.9	24.9
Industry Rank	---	48	83	3	7	7

Industry Rank (100=Worst)

ROE Breakdown

	1995	1996	1997	1998	1999	TTM
Net Margin%	-6.5	3.7	-28.0	13.3	14.7	14.7
Asset Turnover	1.4	1.0	1.1	1.5	1.2	1.2
Financial Leverage	NMF	1.2	1.7	1.5	1.5	1.5

View company's full financials

Financial Health Grade: A   What is this?
Fiscal year-end: December   Qtr = Current Quarter

	1995	1996	1997	1998	1999	Qtr
Long-Term Debt $Mil	---	---	---	---	---	---
Total Equity $Mil	-13	33	27	54	113	134
Debt/Equity	---	---	---	---	---	---
S&P 500	0.6	0.8	0.7	1.7	0.8	1.1
Financial Leverage	NMF	1.2	1.7	1.5	1.5	1.5
S&P 500	4.5	4.8	4.6	4.9	4.9	5.4
Current Ratio	---	---	---	2.9	2.7	2.6
S&P 500	1.5	1.7	1.7	1.6	1.5	1.6

View balance sheet

Valuation Grade: B   What is this?
Fiscal year-end: December   TTM = Trailing 12 Months

	1995	1996	1997	1998	1999	TTM
Price/Earnings	---	---	NMF	48.4	78.6	105.6
Price/Book	---	---	4.3	14.0	20.4	25.1
Price/Sales	---	---	2.3	6.5	11.5	14.9
Price/Cash Flow	---	---	NMF	282.9	59.7	82.5
Appraisal Ratio	---	---	---	---	---	0.8

Appraisal Ratio > 1.0 = Undervalued
Appraisal Ratio < 1.0 = Overvalued

CHAPTER 10

Technical Screening, Back Testing, and Model Creation

Most professionals use technical trading models only as a timing aid. The buy and sell signals generated by these models assist them in entering into and exiting from positions that they favor for other reasons. But some types of traders depend on technicals more than others; a futures trader in the bond pit at the CBOT is more likely to give more weight to charts and indicators than will a portfolio manager at a value fund. There are even a few traders who religiously execute every trade recommended by their favorite model.

There are hundreds of technical trading models, and the Internet allows traders to examine every buy and sell signal generated by the model of their choice—past and present. But in reviewing these models for possible use, a trader must not be unduly impressed by the results of some *back tests*: tests of the profitability of the model if applied to historic data. Some analytic models have so many "degrees of freedom" in statistical terms (where the user can set several parameters that define the model), an analyst could create a version of the model that identified every past high and low of any security. Statisticians would call this "overfitting" the predictive model to past reality.

Professional traders understand that some models work better in certain markets: in trending markets better than in trading ranges, in high volatility better than in low. A trader considering use of a particular model should also review the risk in adhering to its rules. Some models require that their devotees have staying power: They must be able to ride out a series of bad signals before the system kicks in again with good ones.

The simplest charting techniques are most likely to work, because their success can be explained in terms of repetitive human behavior. Similarly, the best analytic techniques can be vetted using the same criteria. For example, a method that generates a buy signal because of a recent rapid price increase may be picking up on a psychological imbalance in favor of greed over fear. Or it might be picking up on buy orders by traders with information of which most are not yet aware. Technicians must understand the reason why a method has been successful in the past before they can rely on it to perform just as well in the future.

For stocks in particular, a trader must be sufficiently well acquainted with company fundamentals in order to understand whether there are any good and valid reasons for a particular technical anomaly. Then, the trader can be more confident in identifying that a stock's price is rich or cheap instead of just high or low.

CHAPTER 10 Technical Screening, Back Testing, and Model Creation   163

USING BACK-TESTED SEARCHES BASED ON TECHNICAL DATA

Source: WallStreetCity.com

Price: Premium

FIGURE 10-1

ProSearch Technical Search and Back Test from WallStreetCity

Top 25 best purchase candidates -- 15-20 min Quote Delay.

Symbol	Name	Group	Options	Trend	Price	10Brk	21Brk	30Brk	Mc8d	BMc12BMn
DIMC	DIMECO INC			↑	29.000	↑	↑	↑	↑	↑
SBSI	SOUTHSIDE BANCSHARES INC	BAN		↑	8.750	↑	↑	↑		
ANTV	ANTENNA TV SA ADR SPONSORED	BTV		↑	15.250	↑	↑	↑	↑	↑
ZBRA	ZEBRA TECHNOLOGIES CORP CL A	DCS	Options	↑	51.000	↑	↑	↑	↑	
FBF	FLEETBOSTON FINL CORP	BAN	Options	↑	37.562	↑	↑	↑		↑
ASPX	AUSPEX SYS INC	DCS	Options	↑	5.562	↑	↑	↑	↑	↑
TCBA	TARPON COAST BANCORP INC			↑	9.500	↑	↑	↑	↑	↑
SABH	SAN BENITO BK HOLLISTER CA			↑	15.000	↑	↑	↑	↑	
CERN	CERNER CORP	EIC	Options	↑	32.750	↑	↑	↑	↑	↑
CBBI	CB BANCSHARES INC	BAN		↑	25.250	↑	↑	↑	↑	
ABIL	AMERICABILIA COM INC			↑	10.250	↑	↑	↑		
T.BCC	ACLINICHEM DEV INC CL A			↓	16.700		↑		↑	↑
JDSU	JDS UNIPHASE CORP	TES	Options	↑	123.562	↑	↑	↑	↑	
VRSN	VERISIGN INC	INT	Options	↑	180.500	↑	↑	↑		
PENN	PENN NATL GAMING INC	LRT	Options	↑	14.937	↑	↑	↑	↑	
BOBJ	BUSINESS OBJECTS S A ADR SPONSORED	DSO	Options	↑	92.000	↑	↑	↑		↑
T.JDU	JDS UNIPHASE CDA LTD EXCH NV SHS			↑	182.350	↑	↑	↑		
UGS	UNIGRAPHICS SOLUTIONS INC CL A	DSO		↓	16.937				↑	↑
ANTX	ANTEX BIOLOGICS INC	DBI		↑	8.590	↑	↑			
FUBK	FUTURA BANC CORP			↑	22.500	↑	↑	↑		

WallStreetCity.com allows the user to screen stocks based on technical as well as fundamental criteria.

The search of Figure 10-1 identifies the best purchase candidates, based on bullish signals from the greatest number of indicators (many more columns of indicators are not shown). If the user clicks on one of the indicators, WallStreetCity generates a chart detailing the performance of the model based on that indicator.

For example, Figure 10–2 shows a one-year chart of Dimeco Inc. based on the simplest version of the 10-day Moving Average Breakout method. This method is one of the simplest technical indicators: If the price of the stock trades above its 10-day moving average, a buy signal is generated, and if it trades back below the average, a sell signal is generated. This model is never neutral; one always has either a long or short position.

The arrows on the chart show the timing of the buy and sell signals for the last year (the user can select other time periods, as well, including as far back in history as the data allows). The loss of 150 percent over 25 trades shows that this model has performed badly, and the price chart shows why.

The Moving Average Breakout method is meant to identify changes in trend: It works best on securities that tend to move steadily in one direction for prolonged periods of time. But it will fail if applied to a security that oscillates instead of trends, as does Dimeco. It will buy *rich* on each upward spike, and sell *cheap* on each downward spike.

CHAPTER 10 Technical Screening, Back Testing, and Model Creation **165**

FIGURE 10-2

Chart of Moving Average Breakout Criteria for Dimeco Inc. on July 20, 2000, from WallStreetCity

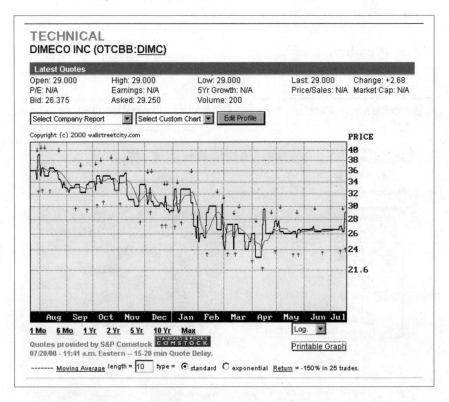

SEARCHES BASED ON OPTION PARAMETERS

Source: WallStreetCity.com

Price: Premium

FIGURE 10-3

ProSearch Option Model Definition from WallStreetCity

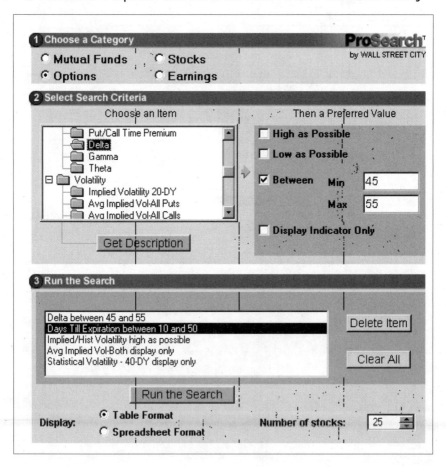

CHAPTER 10   Technical Screening, Back Testing, and Model Creation   **167**

WallStreetCity allows the user to screen options based on those technical criteria specific to options. Daily, WallStreetCity calculates numerous option statistics, including time value, days to expiration, volatilities (both historical and implied), and "the Greeks":[1] measures of the sensitivity of the price of the option to the price of the variables on which it depends.

The most useful among these statistics are the volatilities. WallStreetCity calculates three types: *implied* (that volatility that would statistically imply that the value of the option is equal to its current market price), *statistical* (the volatility calculated from historical prices of the underlying security), and *historical* (in WallStreetCity's definition, an average value for past statistical volatilities). The values for statistical and historical volatility depend on the number of past days used to compute them, and WallStreetCity offers shorter-term and longer-term choices. In practice, it uses the average of up to 1 1/2 years of past 20-day statistical volatilities when it calculates its historical volatility.

The search specified in Figure 10–3 is intended to identify options for which the Implied/Historical Ratio is as high as possible. Since implied volatility is forward looking, and historical volatility is backward looking, searching for options with this criteria will identify those stocks that options traders expect will move more in the future than they have in the past.

Two additional criteria were added. First, days to expiration was required to be between 10 and 50 days. And second, the *delta* of the option (an options statistic that indicates the sensi-

---

[1] So denoted because they are named for Greek letters: delta, gamma, theta, vega, and rho.

tivity of the price of the option to the price of the underlying security) must be between 45 and 55. This criterion requires that all the options selected must be close to at-the-money; that is, their strike price must be close to the current market price of the stock.

For example, the delta of an at-the-money option is about 50 percent; statistically, it is 50 percent likely that the option will be exercised if market movement is random. For small price moves, the price of the option will rise $0.50 for each $1 increase in the price of the stock. The delta of an option is not a constant: It changes as a function of time, volatility, and price. The delta of a very far out-of-the-money option goes to 0 percent, and the delta of a very far in-the-money option goes to 100 percent.

The days to expiration and delta criteria were added in large part to ensure that the results of the search are meaningful and executable. If an option has very little time to expiration, or if it's very far in- or out-of-the-money, the implied volatilities may be almost meaningless. For instance, pricing an option on its close (as is done by WallStreetCity) instead of the bid side may double the implied volatility if the option is only worth 1/16.

The results of the search are shown in Figure 10–4. The option with the highest Implied/Historical Ratio of 1051 percent is the August 15 Call on First Security Corp. (FSCO). Note that the option is close to at-the-money: its Delta is 0.481, and it has 29 days to expiration.

A click on the stock symbol reveals the price history of the option and its underlying stock shown in Figure 10–5. This chart reveals some peculiar patterns.

CHAPTER 10   Technical Screening, Back Testing, and Model Creation   **169**

FIGURE 10-4

ProSearch Option Search Results from WallStreetCity

Search Results

- Copy all symbols into a portfolio   • Display table without criteria values

Top 25 best-fit matches — 15-20 min Quote Delay.

Symbol	Name	Group	Stock	Price	Delta	DyExp	IV:HV	Av/VB	40SVo
FBZ HC	FSCO AUG 19, 2000 $ 15.000 CALL	BAN	FSCO	11.875	$0.481	29	1051%	161.2	42.2
RDW HF	BRCM AUG 19, 2000 $ 130.000 CALL	INT	BRCM	100.625	$0.547	29	525%	102.9	69.1
HWF HE	HWP AUG 19, 2000 $ 125.000 CALL	DAT	HWP	19.750	$0.514	29	320%	70.8	45.5
PLL HD	PLL AUG 19, 2000 $ 20.000 CALL	MFC	PLL	1.812	$0.489	29	227%	67.8	35.3
FBR HU	FBR AUG 19, 2000 $ 7.500 CALL	FMB	FBR	0.906	$0.510	29	195%	147.8	63.6
AIS HW	AMPL AUG 19, 2000 $ 17.500 CALL	INV	AMPL	2.249	$0.498	29	194%	140.2	82.7
FBR TU	FBR AUG 19, 2000 $ 7.500 PUT	FMB	FBR	0.968	$0.490	29	190%	147.8	63.6
UMI TV	MGIC AUG 19, 2000 $ 12.500 PUT	DSO	MGIC	2.125	$0.548	29	187%	105.5	60.4
FXQ HU	FVCX AUG 19, 2000 $ 7.500 CALL	DCS	FVCX	1.250	$0.549	29	185%	114.9	90.4
LE HH	LE AUG 19, 2000 $ 40.000 CALL	RMC	LE	4.437	$0.550	29	184%	95.7	51.3

First, the stock lost half its value early in March 2000. And second, the price of the stock has been relatively stable for the past three months. As Figure 10–4 shows, the 40-day statistical volatility is 42.2 percent, while the implied volatility is 161.2 percent; traders expect the future to be four times more volatile than the recent past.

Clearly, First Security's fundamentals must be responsible for both the past actual volatility and the future expected volatility. The Research Wizard feature of MSN.com speeded the investigation of the fundamentals.

Research Wizard is an *expert system:* that is, an automated system that mimics the advice or actions of a bona-fide expert. It attempts to answer key questions about fundamentals, price history, price targets, and catalysts for each security. In addition, it compares a stock to others in its industry, and uses that comparison in some of its projections.

FIGURE 10-5

Details about Option and Underlying Security from WallStreetCity

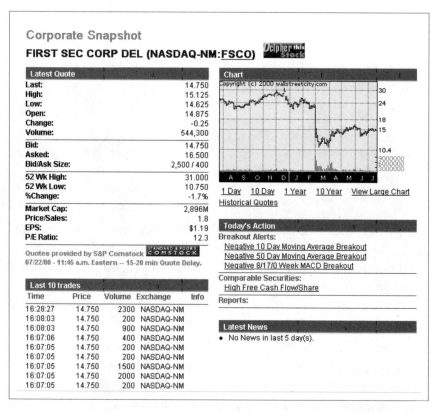

Figure 10-6 shows a partial listing of catalysts called Alerts for First Security. The text of the news alerts reveals the reason for the past behavior:

"When the Company revealed, on March 3, 2000, that its operating results for the fourth fiscal quarter would fall short of estimates, the price of First Security common stock dropped by 38 percent, falling from $22.50 per share, to $13.968 per share."

CHAPTER 10 Technical Screening, Back Testing, and Model Creation 171

FIGURE 10-6

Research Wizard Alerts for First Security Corp. as of July 22, 2000, from MSN

Price/Volume alerts		
05/30/00	**Relative price strength** increasing.	Chart	Description
Analyst alerts		
04/25/00	FSCO : **Coverage Initiated by Warburg Dillon Read:** **Hold** -.	Ratings Calendar	Description
Calendar event alerts		
07/20/00	FSCO has notified the SEC of an **unscheduled material event**.	Description
05/17/00	**Significant share of ownership** report filed with SEC.	Edgar Filings for this Company	Description
04/19/00	**Significant share of ownership** report filed with SEC.	Edgar Filings for this Company	Description
Financial alerts		
05/17/00	0.14 **dividend paid**.	Description
News alerts		
07/18/00	FSCO **announced earnings**: "First Security Corporation Announces Second Quarter Results Highlights: - Excluding the major unusu...."	Read News Item	Description

And it reveals the reason for the high implied volatility, as well:

"On April 10, 2000, First Security and Wells Fargo & Company (WFC) announced the signing of a definitive agreement to merge. . . . A special meeting of First Security stockholders has been scheduled for July 31, 2000, to vote on the merger."

Note that this meeting is scheduled to occur before the option expires. Often, when an event of paramount importance is on the horizon, the price of a security will trade in a narrow range while waiting for the trigger event. But the price of the security is virtually certain to move substantially on the news; a vote on a merger is an on-or-off event; there is no neutral outcome. Together, the option technicals and the stock fundamentals provide all traders—not just options traders—much insight about market expectations for the price of First Security.

CHAPTER 10 Technical Screening, Back Testing, and Model Creation   173

VISUAL SCREENING FOR REAL-TIME TRADE IDEAS

Source: FalconEye.com

Price: Premium

F I G U R E 10–7

Tracker as of July 21, 2000, from FalconEye

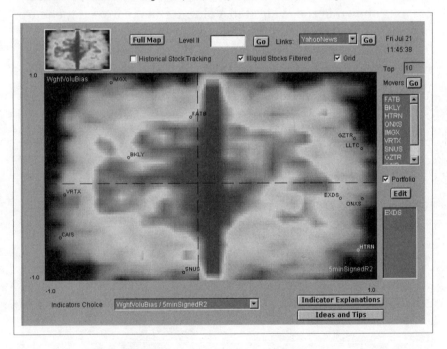

"Tracker" from FalconEye.com allows the user to screen all 6500 Nasdaq stocks for exceptional real-time behavior. Because Figure 10–7 is shown in shades of gray, it doesn't do justice to Tracker. Tracker's Stock Cloud is really a three-dimensional chart, where color coding represents the third dimension: the density (number of observations) at each point on the x-y axis. Red represents the greatest density (most stocks) at a pair of coordinates, while light blue represents the lowest density (least stocks). Tracker shows the location within the cloud of the top movers and any securities in the user's portfolio.

The user selects predefined indicators as the horizontal and vertical axes. FalconEye designed each of these indicators, and has back-tested their value as a trading aid. The default vertical axis shown is the Weighted Volume Bias index—a measure of the relative strength of the bid side versus the offer side.[2] The default horizontal axis is the 5 Minute Signed R^2 index: a measure of the relative strength of the trend over the last five minutes.

FIGURE 10-8

Tracker Interpretations from FalconEye

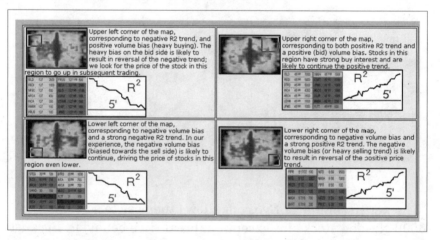

---

[2] The exact calculation is shown if the Indicator Explanations button is clicked.

CHAPTER 10   Technical Screening, Back Testing, and Model Creation   **175**

Figure 10–8 shows possible interpretations of Tracker's results. For example, stocks in the upper right corner of the cloud have both a bullish order book and a recent upward trend, making them potential buy candidates.

To identify breakaway stocks that are present in that region, the user can zoom in on a part of the cloud and find which stocks are present in that area. If the Historical Stock Tracking option is selected, FalconEye will plot the behavior of the selected securities, and the user can watch those stocks move about the cloud as time passes.

CHAPTER 11

Expert Opinions and Recommendations

Not every professional investor is a skilled financial analyst or a money market economist. And only those at the largest funds have the kind of access to companies that the top Wall Street analysts enjoy. Therefore, traders depend on the opinions of analysts they respect.

An analyst's job is not all facts and figures. The analyst visits the companies, meets management, tours facilities, and gets a qualitative impression of the company's prospects to supplement the quantitative facts. The analyst participates in conference calls scheduled by the company for institutional investors and analysts, and frequently talks to the company, its suppliers, and its customers.

A public company will roll out the red carpet for a top analyst, hoping for recommendations that will enhance the price of its stock. By giving a recommendation, the analyst has the power to move markets, as do the most well-known fund managers. But before using outside advice, an individual investor must determine the qualifications of the advisor and identify the advisor's objectives. Expert advice is the antithesis of chat room talk, where an investor can't know the identity, qualifications, or motives of those who post remarks.

For example, many of the top analysts are employed by broker/dealers who also serve as investment bankers to the same companies they cover. Although these analysts may be perceived to have a conflict of interest and are likely to be biased in favor of a company that provides their employer with millions of dollars of revenue, they are also perceived as more knowledgeable about that company than their competitors.

Often, prominent portfolio managers appear on television to comment on a stock. Their case can be compelling and can influence price instantly. But investors must be aware that the reason for their appearance is almost always to tout a position they already have; it's unreasonable to think they would let their comments drive up the price of a stock they have yet to buy.

CHAPTER 11   Expert Opinions and Recommendations

REVIEWING ANALYSTS' OPINIONS

Source: MultexInvestor.com

Price: Free and Premium

FIGURE 11-1

Summary of Brokerage Recommendations on July 20, 2000, for Exodus Communications from MultexInvestor

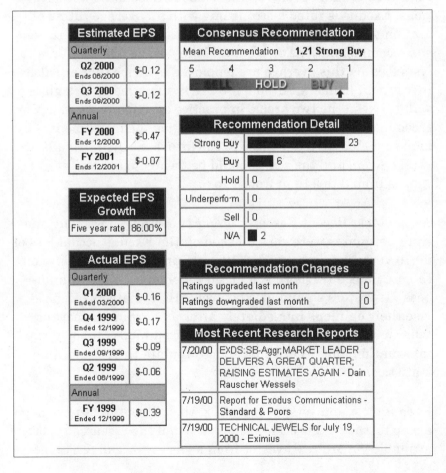

Multex.com is a site dedicated to fundamental investment research for individual and institutional investors. MultexInvestor.com is the half of Multex.com that individual investors are allowed to access. MultexInvestor provides consensus estimates of earnings, growth rates, and analysts' recommendations, as well as a listing of the most recent research reports.

Figure 11-1 summarizes opinions about Exodus Communications. Exodus is rated a strong buy with an average rating of 1.21 on a scale of 1 to 5. However, investors must grade consensus recommendations on a curve. Many of the research analysts feeding this average are employed by firms that are also investment bankers. Although there is supposed to be a glass wall between the two areas, in practice a company given a poor recommendation may be less likely to give the investment banker its lucrative business in the future. So "sell" signals are rarely given, and the scale should be treated more as if it ranges from 3 to 5 than from 1 to 5.

As the Most Recent Research Reports section shows, one analyst's estimates were raised based on the Exodus actual loss of $0.10 versus estimates of $0.12, announced after the close on the previous day (there is a lag in reporting the latest numbers). Investors should also be aware that analysts often revise their opinions immediately after an earnings report or other news. Many do so to adjust their opinions for the new information, but others do it to manipulate their performance statistics.

Even if most analysts favor a stock, the diligent investor will go a step further. Figure 11-2 shows a list of the research reports available via MultexInvestor from a variety of sources. Some

CHAPTER 11 Expert Opinions and Recommendations   181

FIGURE 11-2

Research Reports Available for Exodus on
July 20, 2000, from MultexInvestor

Most recent reports on Exodus Communications Inc, Santa Clara Ca	More on EXDS ▶ Research Earnings Chart/Quote Snapshot Stock Talk

Free and Sponsored Reports

	7/17/00	TECHNOLOGY:ML Tech Bits & Bytes 7/17 PM *Merrill Lynch Private Client* - 2 pages	Merrill Lynch
	7/17/00	EXODUS COMM.:Exodus Turns to Better Deal with Digex *Merrill Lynch Private Client* - 2 pages	Merrill Lynch
🔍	7/15/00	Stock Snapshot -- Exodus Communications *Multex-Stock Snapshot* - 3 pages - Free	
🔍	7/15/00	ACE Consensus Estimates -- Exodus Communications *Multex-ACE Consensus Estimates* - 2 pages - Free	
🔍	5/29/00	ThePerspective - Weekly Insights From Deutsche Banc Alex. Brown *Deutsche Banc Alex. Brown - US Equities* - 54 pages	Deutsche Banc Alex. Brown
🔍	5/26/00	Exodus Communications - Company Update - Earnings Forecast and/or Target Price Change *Morgan Stanley Dean Witter Research* - 2 pages	MORGAN STANLEY DEAN WITTER
	4/24/00	EXDS: Profitability, But 4Q99 Makes Tough 1Q00 Revenue Comparable *Salomon Smith Barney Online* - Morning Note	SALOMON SMITH BARNEY A member of citigroup

are free, and others are sold for a fee. The user can preview thumbnail versions of those reports flagged with a magnifying glass before download or purchase.

Reports such as these generally provide the investor with insight into the analyst's logic, as well as extensive quantitative data that backs up the analyst's opinion. Besides giving the investor additional color about the company, such reports also serve as an indication of future conditions that might persuade the analyst to upgrade or downgrade the stock.

QUALIFYING ANALYSTS' OPINIONS

Source: BulldogResearch.com

Price: Free

FIGURE 11-3

Snapshot of Opinions about Exodus Communications from BulldogResearch

BulldogResearch.com's stated mission is to "track every analyst, every stock, every industry, every day." In practice this means that BulldogResearch tracks all research analysts that appear in the I/B/E/S International Inc. database of analyst forecasts. This database includes more than 3000 analysts from more than 350 different research firms. A few of the major broker/dealers do not contribute to this database, but most do.

Figure 11-3 shows the BulldogResearch Company Snapshot for Exodus Communications, Inc. on July 18, 2000, the day before

CHAPTER 11 Expert Opinions and Recommendations   **183**

it released second quarter earnings. It details the Exodus consensus recommendation, its 12-month price target, its earnings estimate, and other statistics.

As Figure 11–4 shows, BulldogResearch allows the user to link to a report that provides the names of the top analysts, as well as a history of revisions to earnings estimates. BulldogResearch.com bestows Bulldog Awards on those analysts with a track record of successful predictions. The Award Winners History includes only analysts who have won a Bulldog Award for at least one stock or industry.

FIGURE 11–4

Detail of Earnings Estimates for Exodus Communications as of July 18, 2000, from BulldogResearch

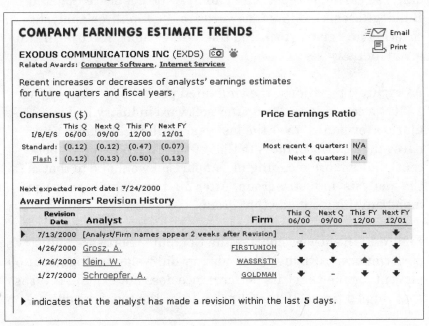

A trader might use this information to skew the trader's personal estimate of earnings toward that of the analysts who have been most accurate in their recent predictions or those analysts the trader particularly respects. (Depending upon which firm employs the analyst, individual investors may find the predictions easy or difficult to obtain.)

The Bulldog Awards are based solely on proprietary mathematical algorithms that measure accuracy, consistency, and performance by simulating the return on a theoretical portfolio for each analyst. They contain no subjective element. When an analyst recommends a stock, it is added to the theoretical portfolio. And if the analyst turns neutral or bearish, the stock is sold.

BulldogResearch uses the return on this theoretical portfolio as one of the award criteria. Awards and rankings are updated daily, as earnings reports and analyst forecasts are updated. BulldogResearch limits its awards to the top three analysts covering any given stock and the top five analysts covering any given industry.

As Figure 11–5 shows, the simulated portfolios of the top five analysts covering the computer software industry had spectacular performances over the last year. BulldogResearch compares their performances to that of the S&P 500 (up 28 percent), but a more meaningful comparison would be to that of the analysts' industry group. After all, they can never recommend anything outside that group.

Figure 11–6 shows a chart of the Computer Software industry's performance. Although the industry did well (gaining about 50 percent for the year), its performance does not explain returns that ranged from 419 to 901 percent for the top five analysts.

CHAPTER 11 Expert Opinions and Recommendations

FIGURE 11-5

Industry Stock Picking Awards for Computer Software from BulldogResearch

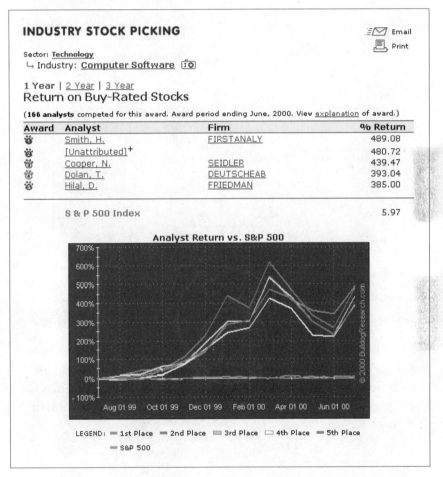

Clearly, skill was involved. But risk was involved as well. Note that each of the five analysts took a major hit starting at the beginning of March 2000. An individual investor who mirrored the theoretical portfolio with real dollars might have lost

FIGURE 11-6

Chart of Computer Software as of July 18, 2000, from BigCharts

nearly 60 percent by starting a program on March 1 and leaving it on June 1. But Figure 11–4 shows no such *draw-down* (loss following a high-water mark of profits), which implies that the top-performing analysts tend to recommend high-volatility stocks.

GETTING THE FULL STORY

Source: StreetEvents.com

Price: Free

FIGURE 11–7

Listing of Audio Events for July 19, 2000, from StreetEvents

Upcoming Earnings Releases

Company Name	Ticker	Date	Time (ET)
ACNielsen	ART	7-19	
Aspect Medical Systems	ASPM	7-19	
Banco Latinoamericano de Exportaciones	BLX	7-19	
Interpore	BONZ	7-19	
Credit Acceptance	CACC	7-19	
Columbia Bancorp	CBMD	7-19	

To listen to the multimedia event, click on the Full Page

Live Conference Call Webcasts

Company Name	Ticker	Date	Time (ET)
EMC	EMC	7-19	8:15am
Tellabs	TLAB	7-19	8:15am
MapInfo	MAPS	7-19	8:30am
Alltel Corporation	AT	7-19	8:30am
Tricon Global Restaurants	YUM	7-19	9:00am
ESPS	ESPS	7-19	9:00am

To listen to the multimedia event, click on the Full Page

StreetEvents.com provides the serious investor with the ability to listen to conference calls sponsored by companies and broker/dealers.

Conference calls are one mechanism by which a company manages its investor relations. Often, it will hold a conference call to announce earnings or other material events. Sometimes it does so to manage bad news, such as an accounting revision. At a conference call, the company will often discuss the factors behind its financial results as well as its outlook for its sector and its plans for the future. Usually the conference call includes a question-and-answer period limited to professionals.

A serious investor gets more color about the company from a conference call than from a dry reading of its prepared press releases. Tone of voice can reveal much. Also, the type of questions asked by analysts—and the quality of the company's answers—can give the investor insight into how the company's most recent announcements are being received by institutional investors.

Previously, participation in conference calls was limited to industry professionals. When the calls were carried out over phone lines, participants were supplied with a phone number and a pass code that allowed them access to the conference. Individual investors were not permitted to participate, for fear that the conference would become unmanageable.

Now, although many conference calls are still restricted, the Internet allows others to be broadcast as Web casts. StreetEvents offers Web casts to both institutional and retail investors. Figure 11–7 shows the StreetEvents calendar of upcoming events, as well as links to live conference calls. It also allows the user to listen to archived conference calls.

CHAPTER 11 Expert Opinions and Recommendations   189

GETTING EXPERT TECHNICAL COMMENTARY

Source: TradingMarkets.com

Price: Premium

FIGURE 11-8
Expert Comment on AM S&P Futures Activity on July 20, 2000, from TradingMarkets

---

Borsellino's S&Ps A.M.

Mr. Greenspan, You Were Saying???
By Lewis J. Borsellino
July 20, 2000 9:20 AM EST

U.S. markets will be keenly attuned to what Mr. Greenspan has to say as Humphrey-Hawkins Testimony begins. If he would like to know what to do, he could just ask anybody who's trading these days.... We'll see what happens.

As for S&Ps this morning, futures were traading before the opening at 1499.80, down 50. On the upside, to get out of immediate trouble, S&Ps must get above 1506.50, then not go below 1503.50. If that happens, they should try for the 1513-1515 area, and possibly 1519.

On the downside, if S&Ps trade below 1495, then can't get over 1498, they should be headed for 1490, 1488 and 1486.50-1486.

A crucial pivot point comes in at 1502.50. 1486.30 is a one and a half week low (last Tuesday). The 100-day moving average comes in at 1476.90. The 50-day at 1473.50. 1458.50 is the 200-day moving average. The market obviously is trading comfortably above all these moving averages. The weekly high made on Monday at 1533 was a three and one quarter month high.

TradingMarkets.com provides "guru" commentary for a variety of markets. The user can also request email alerts and summaries of market action.

FIGURE 11-9

Daily Tick Chart for Sep 2000 S&P 500 Futures from eSignal

In Figure 11–8, Lewis Borsellino discusses important chart points for the S&P futures contract. And as Figure 11–9 shows, his commentary was practically a road map of price action for the rest of the day.

PART FOUR
Risk, Reward, and Performance Measurement

The skill that demarcates the professional investor from the amateur more than any other is the ability to manage market risk. Risk is not a bad thing; it is merely uncertainty about outcome. And when thinking about future market moves, the professional always forecasts the full range of possible outcomes—both positive and negative—instead of just the individual's expectation.

Before writing a ticket, the professional determines that risk is bounded to an appropriate level. The professional anticipates the worst scenario and has a plan of action for both adverse and beneficial market moves. One of the best traders on the floor of the CBOT always writes two tickets—at least mentally—when entering a new position: one to exit the position at a profit, and one to exit the position at a loss.

Even the most risk-prone institutions limit their risk—albeit to high levels. In the trading room, every trader has risk limits set by management that determine the size and nature of the positions taken. First and foremost, management must be confident that its risk positions do not jeopardize the continued existence of the firm.

But each trader must also optimize his or her risk/reward profile. The professional trader must ensure that the risk currency is spent wisely and that there are no better choices than the trade under consideration—one choice being waiting for a better trade.

For portfolio managers, optimization is a particularly difficult task. One of the devices that they use to limit portfolio risk is diversification. Ideally, when some of securities in the portfolio trade down, others will trade up, thus reducing the size of the loss on the worst days.

But the benefit of diversification depends on the degree of interaction between the securities in the portfolio. Even if the portfolio contains 100 different securities, diversification will provide no benefit if they all trade up and down together. In fact, it will do harm: The portfolio is mostly invested in securities that were not the portfolio manager's first choice based on expected return.

The number of possible combinations for a portfolio is mind-boggling. So professionals depend on sophisticated mathematical tools to aid them in optimizing the structure of their portfolio.

The next two chapters discuss how traders use such tools to measure market risk, to control that risk, and to optimize their risk/reward profile for various types of positions. They also discuss how portfolio managers analyze the actual performance of a portfolio after the fact, and determine the reasons for its success or failure relative to expectations.

CHAPTER 12

Risk Measurement

Risk measurement serves two purposes in the trading room. First, it provides an objective measure of risk that trading management can use to ensure that individual traders, product areas, and the firm as a whole remain within risk limits. And second, it allows trading management to evaluate performance in light of the risk taken to achieve it.

The investing public judges mutual and hedge funds by the same standards. A fund is rewarded for outstanding returns with new investments. But it's penalized for achieving those returns at the expense of high risk, as measured by statistics such as *Beta* (the volatility of returns relative to an index such as the S&P 500). Most individuals are risk averse: They would prefer a guaranteed 10 percent return on their investments to a 1 to 21 percent range of returns. So a fund with good returns and low volatility will likely attract more new money than a fund with spectacular returns and high volatility.

THE RISK MEASUREMENT PROCESS

It's not very difficult for an astute trader to estimate the risk of a single security. By examining historical charts, the past volatility of the security can be used as the first approximation of its future volatility. And by staying aware of upcoming catalytic events, the trader can tweak this approximation to be forward looking rather than backward looking.

But a position that includes more than one security is another matter. A portfolio is different from the sum of its positions: Depending on the degree of correlation between the securities in the portfolio, it may act like an entirely different animal.

To measure the risk of a portfolio, traders and mathematicians use a variety of devices. The simplest is to simulate the performance of the portfolio in the past. Such a simulation will automatically pick up on any relationships among the securities in the portfolio, and can often reveal unique patterns.

But studying the past isn't enough. Although everything that *has* happened can happen again, everything that *can* happen has not necessarily yet happened. As the disclaimers read: "Past results are no guarantee of future performance."

So, mathematicians have built statistical models to estimate future portfolio risk. Unlike historical simulation, a statistically based model allows some chance of events that have never been seen before.

Most risk measurement models use statistics taken from recent history in quantifying risk. For example, most use the historical volatilities of *each security* in the portfolio as well as the past correlation between *each pair* of securities in the portfolio in their calculations. Use of such statistics implicitly forecasts that the future will be similar to the past.

CHAPTER 12 Risk Measurement

THE TOOLS

Until very recently, individual investors had no access to analytic tools that would allow them to evaluate the risk/reward profile of a portfolio. These tools were available only to institutions, and were so mathematically complex that only the most quantitative professionals could understand the theory or the results.

Now, risk measurement models intended for the individual investor are available over the Internet. The same individuals who built risk management systems for Street and institutional use are the creators of these Web sites, and they have done a very credible job making their sites more accessible and understandable by amateurs.

RISK AS A FORECAST

Nevertheless, the individual investor should not use these sites as if they were a "black box" that spits out results that can be trusted implicitly. Although it's not necessary to understand the mathematical theory, each user must be aware of the assumptions about market behavior on which the results depend. Then, if for some reason the assumptions appear to be flawed, the investor knows that the results of the risk analysis are as well.

For instance, the most important assumption intrinsic to most models is that the future is best represented by the past; that future volatility, for example, will be similar to that of the past; or that negative correlation observed between two securities will continue. The models are implicitly making a forecast about the future—forecasts of volatility and behavior rather than price, but forecasts nonetheless.

An investor who has reason to doubt this assumption must take the results of the models with a grain of salt. And the investor must always keep in mind that a model based on historical statistics will never forecast conditions that have never been seen before.

TRACKING PORTFOLIO PERFORMANCE

Source: MSN.com

Price: Free

FIGURE 12-1

Return Analysis for Custom Portfolio from MSN

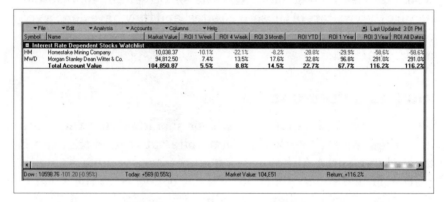

Using this tool, MSN.com provides the trader with the ability to monitor multiple portfolios. The user can create and update a portfolio by entering transactions, creating a "watch list," or downloading the current portfolio from one of several on-line brokers.

Figure 12-1 shows one analysis for a portfolio named Interest Rate Dependent Watchlist. It has positions in two stocks: Homestake Mining and Morgan Stanley Dean Witter. Equal principal amounts of each security are assumed to have been purchased three years ago. MSN provides several predefined sets of columns from which the user can choose, such as Value (daily P&L calculations), Quotes, or Return Calculations (as shown in Figure 12–1). Or the user can customize column choices.

The two securities in the portfolio are inversely correlated to each other: that is, when one goes up, the other is expected to go down. This is so because each reacts strongly to interest rates, as well as alternative investment rates such as those available in the stock market.

As a gold mining company, Homestake tends to sell off when expectations for inflation rates drop and gold loses its appeal as an inflation hedge or a safe harbor. And as a broker/dealer, Morgan Stanley tends to rise when expectations for interest rates fall and the stock market does well.

FIGURE 12-2

Chart of Homestake Mining versus Morgan Stanley Dean Witter as of July 21, 2000, from MSN

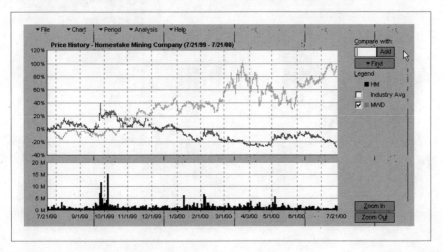

As Figure 12–2 demonstrates, the prices of two companies in apparently unrelated businesses may be correlated to each other if the prices of each strongly depend on the same variables.

MSN allows the user to track the portfolio's value on a daily, weekly, or monthly basis. Figure 12–3 gives the investor an idea of the risk involved in owning this portfolio. For example, the portfolio lost about $14,000, or almost 25 percent, of its value once in 36 months. If this amount of risk is unacceptable, so is the portfolio.

FIGURE 12–3

Price Performance Chart for Custom Portfolio from MSN

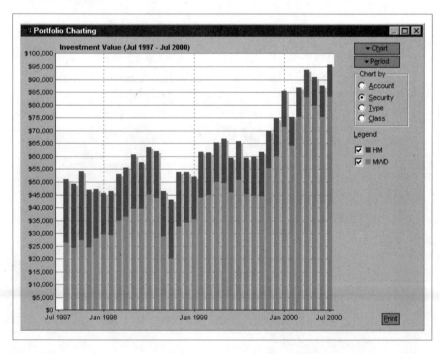

CHAPTER 12 Risk Measurement

One of the best ways to monitor the changing risk of a portfolio is to observe changes in its current market value. MSN allows the user to specify an automatic five-minute frequency for updates; when the value of the portfolio changes dramatically, the investor should investigate the root cause.

MEASURING PORTFOLIO RISK

Source: RiskGrades.com

Price: Premium

FIGURE 12-4

Portfolio Risk Report for Custom Portfolio from RiskGrades

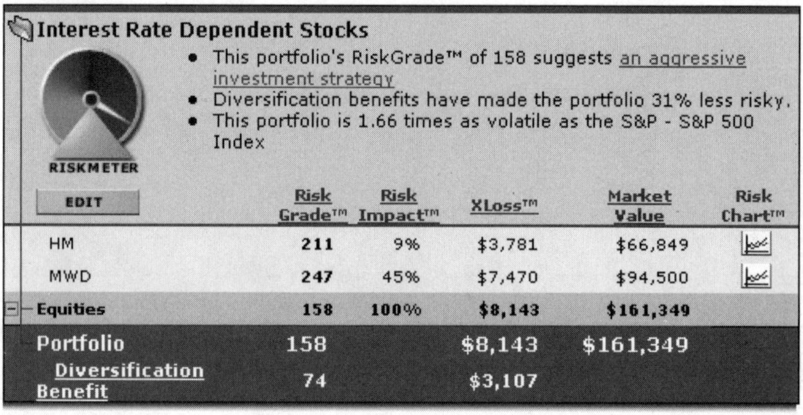

Interest Rate Dependent Stocks
- This portfolio's RiskGrade™ of 158 suggests an aggressive investment strategy
- Diversification benefits have made the portfolio 31% less risky.
- This portfolio is 1.66 times as volatile as the S&P - S&P 500 Index

EDIT	Risk Grade™	Risk Impact™	XLoss™	Market Value	Risk Chart™
HM	211	9%	$3,781	$66,849	
MWD	247	45%	$7,470	$94,500	
Equities	158	100%	$8,143	$161,349	
Portfolio	158		$8,143	$161,349	
Diversification Benefit	74		$3,107		

RiskGrades.com is a product of Risk Metrics. Inc., a firm previously owned by J.P. Morgan that provides risk management software to institutional users.

RiskGrades is a version of Risk Metrics that's intended for use by individual investors. It measures and grades portfolio risk based on statistical calculations of historical prices. As Figure 12–4 shows, RiskGrades considers the Interest Rate Dependent

CHAPTER 12 Risk Measurement

Stocks portfolio previously discussed to be aggressive,[1] being 1.66 times as volatile as the S&P 500.

RiskGrades expresses risk in terms of "Xloss"[2] a statistic that measures the expected one-day loss in the worst five percent of market scenarios. For example, on 95 percent of all days, the Homestake Mining position is expected to either make money or lose less than $3781. RiskGrades calculates XLoss for each security in the portfolio, as well as for the portfolio as a whole.

RiskGrades also calculates exactly how much the portfolio benefits from diversification. Note that the sum of XLoss for the two positions is $11,251 ($3781 + $7470 = $11,351) but the value of XLoss for the portfolio is only $8134. RiskGrades expresses the improvement of $3107 as Diversification Benefit.

Because Homestake Mining is not positively correlated to Morgan Stanley, the chance that the two stocks have their best or worst days together is slight. Portfolio risk will always be less than or equal to the sum of securities risk. Portfolio risk approaches its maximum value when the component securities are positively correlated, and approaches zero when the component securities are negatively correlated.

When designing a portfolio, individual investors must be aware that merely adding additional securities may not significantly reduce risk. Similarly, owning several different mutual funds may not provide much benefit if the funds own the same or similar securities.

---

[1] The portfolio of Figure 12–4 is the same as that used to produce Figure 12–1, except that the sizes of the positions have been reweighted to equal principal value at current market prices.

[2] RiskMinder's "XLoss" is equivalent to *Value at Risk* (VaR), a term more commonly used by risk management experts.

MEASURING RISK FOR OPTIONS ON FUTURES

Source: Optionomics.com

Price: Premium

FIGURE 12-5

Analysis of Options on Bond Futures from Optionomics

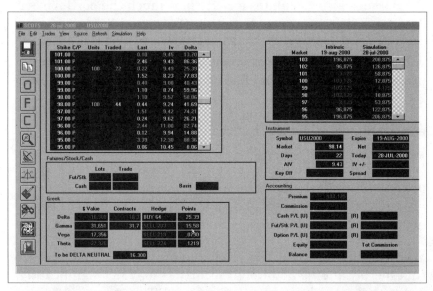

Optionomics.com provides the user with sophisticated analyses of options on stocks and futures. Figure 12-5 shows a composite screen that displays prices,[3] implied volatilities, and risk measurements for options on the September 2000 30-year

---

[3] The prices for bond futures are quoted in 32ds, while the prices of bond options are quoted in 64ths. For example, the price of $1.10 for the 99 Puts is equal to 1 point plus 10/64ths or 1.15625 in decimal.

CHAPTER 12 Risk Measurement

bond contract. Bond futures and their options are both highly liquid, trading at bid/offer spreads generally no larger than 1/32 for size.

The price of an option depends on more than the price of the underlying security, so a trader is at risk from a change in any of the parameters on which the price depends. These parameters include implied volatility, time to expiration, and the risk-free interest rate. Optionomics calculates the sensitivity of the portfolio to each of these variables.

Two options trades have been entered into the system: a buy of one hundred 98 puts and a buy of one hundred 100 calls, at a total cost of $103,125. This position is slightly bearish, because the market price of 98 14/32 is closer to the 98 strike price of the puts than it is to the 100 strike price of the calls. Optionomics calculates the $ Delta of the portfolio to be −$16,300; that is, if the price of the bond rallies one point (and volatility, time, and interest rate remain constant), the position will lose $16,300.

Professional options traders generally bet on the *size* of price moves rather than their *direction*. In this case they would use the value of delta to hedge their position and convert it to a *"long volatility"* position: The traders will make money if the market is more volatile (in either direction) than expected. Optionomics calculates that the options trader must buy 16.3 bond contracts to become *delta neutral*, or insensitive to direction.

The box in the upper right-hand corner simulates the P&L of the position as a function of bond price for two dates: the current date and the expiration date. Note that the position will make $196,000 if the price of the bond at expiration is 103, but will lose the full $103,125 paid for the options if the price of the bond is between the two strike prices of 98 and 100.

MEASURING RISK FOR EQUITY OPTIONS

Source: OmegaResearch.com

Price: Premium

FIGURE 12-6

Risk Report for Options on Microsoft from Optionomics

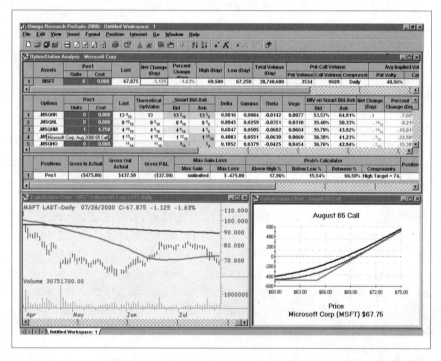

Figure 12-6 shows the types of information a professional options trader might view. OptionStation displays real-time information on trading activity on the underlying security, a historical chart, real-time bid/offer prices on the options, and derived

CHAPTER 12 Risk Measurement

information for each option, including implied volatility calculated on each side of the market.

OptionStation translates market prices to implied volatilities. Note that, depending on the terms of the option, a small change in price can mean a large change in implied volatility. For example, with the price of Microsoft at 67 7/8, the August 55 Calls (MSQHK) are very deep in-the-money. With the option quoted 13 2/16–13 3/8, the bid/offer spread of 1/4 point in price is equal to a bid/offer spread of nearly 10 percent in implied volatility (64.91 percent – 53.57 percent = 9.34 percent).

OptionStation also provides various measures of risk. Take the analysis of "Pos1," a position consisting of one August 65 call. Note that, typical of a long options position, the maximum gain is unlimited while the maximum loss is capped at the cost of the option.

The "Greeks" tell the trader the sensitivity of the price of each option to the price of Microsoft (Delta), to the volatility of each option (Vega), and the passage of time (Theta) at current market prices. (The values of the Greeks are not constant.)

The graph in the lower right describes how profitability depends on the price of Microsoft at three points in time. The classic "hockey puck" shape details the sensitivity of the option to price at expiration, while the smoothest top curve details the sensitivity of the option to an instantaneous change in the price of Microsoft.

ESTIMATING THE RISK OF A TECHNICAL TRADING STRATEGY

Source: TradeStation.com (see also OmegaResearch.com)

Price: Premium

TradeStation.com allows a trader to analyze the risk of any of hundreds of technical trading strategies. The chart of Figure 12–7 indicates every buy and sell signal generated for Microsoft between July 14, 1999, and March 31, 2000, by a *MACD* (Moving Average Crossover) model with the default parameters specified at the top of the chart.

Although the visual history is revealing, TradeStation also quantifies the performance of the model, as shown in Figure 12–8.

In addition to providing meticulous statistics on the winning and losing trades, TradeStation also provides several measures of risk. For example, it details information such as the maximum drawdown (and the volatility of drawdown).

Drawdown provides a trader with some idea of the risk of initiating this MACD-based trading program at exactly the wrong time. This statistic acknowledges that a trader's risk is path-dependent; that is, no matter what the net outcome, the path that performance takes over time must have no pullbacks serious enough to force or scare the trader out.

CHAPTER 12 Risk Measurement

FIGURE 12-7

MACD Strategy Simulation for Microsoft from TradeStation

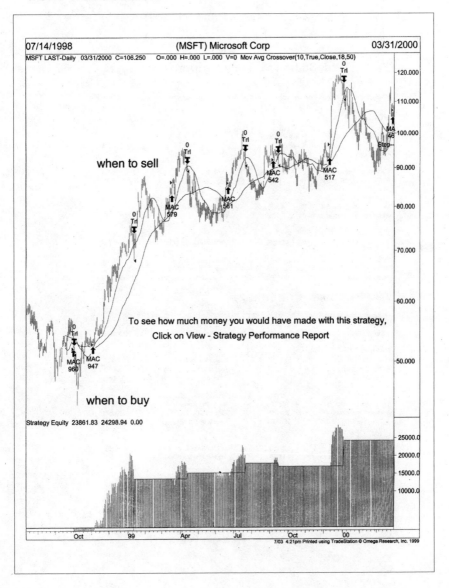

FIGURE 12-8

MACD Strategy Performance Report for Microsoft from TradeStation

Analysis

TradeStation Strategy Performance Report

TradeStation Strategy Performance Report - Mov Avg Crossover MSFT-Daily (7/8/98-3/31/00)

Strategy Analysis

Net Profit	$24,298.94	Open Position	($437.11)
Gross Profit	$26,049.45	Interest Earned	$5,929.63
Gross Loss	($1,750.51)	Commission Paid	$0.00
Percent profitable	66.67%	Profit factor	14.88
Ratio avg. win/avg. loss	7.44	Adjusted profit factor	4.36
Annual Rate of Return	18.79%	Sharpe Ratio	N/A
Return on Initial Capital	24.30%	Return Retracement Ratio	14.81
Return on Max. Drawdown	230.43%	K-Ratio	N/A
Buy/Hold return	104.21%	RINA Index	49.73
Cumulative return	48.65%	Percent in the market	39.65%
Adjusted Net Profit	$10,036.42	Select Net Profit	$24,298.94
Adjusted Gross Profit	$13,024.73	Select Gross Profit	$26,049.45
Adjusted Gross Loss	($2,988.31)	Select Gross Loss	($1,750.51)

Total Trade Analysis

Number of total trades	6		
Average trade	$4,049.82	Avg. trade ± 1 STDEV	$9,951.18 / ($1,851.54)
1 Std. Deviation (STDEV)	$5,901.36	Coefficient of variation	145.72%

Run-up

Maximum Run-up	$22,254.50	Max. Run-up Date	1/8/99
Average Run-up	$7,269.97	Avg. trade ± 1 STDEV	$15,204.21 / $0.00
1 Std. Deviation (STDEV)	$7,934.25	Coefficient of variation	109.14%

Drawdown

Maximum Drawdown	($2,732.30)	Max. Drawdown Date	3/24/99
Average Drawdown	($1,232.30)	Avg. trade ± 1 STDEV	($322.67) / ($2,141.93)
1 Std. Deviation (STDEV)	$909.63	Coefficient of variation	73.82%

Reward/Risk Ratios

Net Prft/Largest Loss	27.59	Net Prft/Max Drawdown	8.89
Adj Net Prft/Largest Loss	11.40	Adj Net Prft/Max Drawdown	3.67

Outlier Trades

	Total Trades	Profit/Loss
Positive outliers	0	$0.00
Negative outliers	0	$0.00
Total outliers	0	$0.00

7/3/00 9:30:06 AM Printed using TradeStation 2000i by Omega Research, Inc. (c) 1999

CHAPTER 13

Portfolio Optimization

There are two approaches toward building a portfolio. The amateur constructs a portfolio from the *bottom up*, buying the stocks that seem attractive and calling the result a portfolio. This is not a portfolio; it's a collection of individual positions.

The professional, on the other hand, constructs a portfolio from the *top down*: It's that combination of securities that produces the optimal mix of risk and reward. Top portfolio managers are valued for their portfolio optimization skills as much as for their market forecasting skills.

The best compliment that a trader can receive from peers is to be called a "money machine." It means the trader generates substantial profits for his or her firm month after month. This pattern of performance is the ideal for the portfolio manager as well. In technical terminology, the portfolio manager attempts to construct a portfolio that will achieve high returns with low volatility. If graphed, the ideal portfolio's performance would show an unvarying trend upward.

PORTFOLIO DESIGN, RESTRUCTURING, AND OPTIMIZATION

Of course, it's difficult for a portfolio manager to find securities with both high return and low volatility. Major market swings are a fact of life for most high fliers. To aid in the search, the portfolio manager might use tools that filter and rank securities by expected return and volatility. Those with the highest return and lowest volatility are those with the optimal *risk premium*; that is, the amount expected will be earned for a given level of risk.

Besides finding the right securities, an astute portfolio manager can control risk by optimizing the composition of the portfolio. If the mix is right, the portfolio manager can include securities with high volatility in a low volatility portfolio.

For example, some portfolio managers search for *securities pairs*; two securities—both with expected high return and volatility—that are negatively correlated to one another. If the relationship holds, when one security is having a bad day, the other will have a good day. Catastrophic risk is minimized, while over time the portfolio will realize the high return of its component securities.

But this process becomes unmanageable when many securities are involved. To aid in the task, a portfolio manager can use *portfolio optimization* tools: mathematical programs that analyze the portfolio and suggest changes to it that improve the risk/reward profile. And after the fact, the portfolio manager can use *performance attribution* tools: programs that determine the reasons for the success or failure of the strategy used.

To optimize portfolio composition, mathematicians generally use models based on the ground-breaking work of Nobel prize-winner Harry Markowitz, the father of *modern portfolio theory*. Markowitz's theory holds that assets should be selected on the basis of how they interact with other assets in a portfolio, and that each manager's objective should be to maximize the return of a portfolio for a given level of risk, or to minimize the level of risk for a given level of return.

In Markowitz's equations, the risk of a portfolio is a mathematical function of three sets of parameters: the size of each position, the volatility of each security, and the correlation between each pair of securities. The larger the positions, the higher the volatility of the securities, and the greater the amount of intercorrelation among those securities, the greater the risk of the portfolio.

The mathematics behind these tools is highly sophisticated, and requires statistical analyses of past performance of every security that might be included in the portfolio. However, some Internet sites now have tools to assist in the process, and have simplified the output to a level understandable by a sophisticated individual investor.

The risk measurement sites provide an objective heads up for those involved in trading particularly risky securities.

WAVE SYSTEMS: A CLASSIC LIQUIDITY SQUEEZE

The *New York Times* relates the story of two brothers in Illinois who invested nearly their entire savings in Wave Systems Corp. (WAVX), a tiny company that creates technologies to safeguard and secure ecommerce data. The brothers rode the price of the stock from $1.00 a share in 1998 to a high of $50.75 on March 1, 2000,[1] and back down to just above $10 a share in April 2000.

The first brother, a teacher of high school physics and economics, had invested $90,000 in Wave over three years. By dedicating nearly all his assets to his Wave position and by leveraging his position to the hilt by margining the stock, he watched the value of his portfolio soar to $2.34 million at the market high. The

---

[1] Danny Hakim, *New York Times,* June 18, 2000.

second brother invested about $35,000, and watched his slightly less leveraged portfolio peak at a market value of $504,000.

The brothers accomplished this spectacular gain by implementing a strategy of zero diversification and maximum leverage. Terrance Odean, a professor at the University of California at Davis who researches investor behavior, pointed out that the brothers' strategy is "the correct formula to maximize the chances for a huge windfall. It's also the correct formula to maximize the chance of losing everything."

The brothers hit both extremes within the course of a single month. On March 29, 2000, the brothers received email margin calls for $221,778 and $43,000, respectively, giving them until April 5 to come up with the cash or risk having their positions forcibly liquidated. The brothers assumed the margin calls were a mistake, because just the previous day Wave had traded at over $50 per share, near its $50.75 high. Further, Wave had hit its high because both the market tone and company fundamentals were good: Nasdaq was up 14 percent for the year, and Wave had just secured $122 million in private financing.

Unbeknown to the two brothers, they had fallen afoul of what risk managers call "event risk," that is, an extraordinary event that creates market instability. In this case, U.S. Clearing, which loaned capital to the brothers' margined accounts, had raised the margin requirement on Wave from 50 to 75 percent. It did so in order to protect itself from margin loan defaults should the price of the stock drop more than 50 percent. Based on Wave's history, U.S. Clearing reasonably concluded that the price of a stock that could rise nearly 500 percent in just three months could drop just as precipitously.

After extensions and attempts to transfer their accounts to a different broker with a lower margin requirement, the first brother liquidated his stock on April 17 at around the opening price of $11 per share, retaining just $64,000 in his brokerage account. The second brother liquidated his stock between $14 and $17 a share, ending the day $14,000 underwater.

THE WARNINGS

In retrospect, Wave was extraordinarily vulnerable to event risk because of the nature of many of its stockholders. The "Wavoids," as they were called, were a virtual club, united in the common purpose of cheering the stock on. They chatted on-line, they phoned each other frequently, and they socialized at board meetings. As the *Times* stated: "Wave has attracted more than 200,000 messages in less than two years, more than the combined chatter on RagingBull.com devoted to Yahoo!, eBay, and America Online."

Surprisingly, the Wavoids are still active; both brothers are again trading Wave exclusively. "Diversification is more or less an excuse for not reading the future," one brother said. "If I had half in an index fund and half in Wave, it would take me ten years to get my capital back instead of five."

MEASURING PORTFOLIO RISK

Source: FinPortfolio.com

Price: Free and Premium

FIGURE 13-1

Custom Portfolio as of July 25, 2000, from FinPortfolio

Ticker	Quantity	Market Price	Market Value	Holding (%)	Gain/Loss	Action
LUV	3304.11	$22.81	$75,375.00	50.00%	$0.00	edit delete
XOM	1000.00	$75.38	$75,375.00	50.00%	$0.00	edit delete
Total			$150,750.00	100.00%		
Add New Asset						
Add New Alert						

Portfolio Notes: Equal principal value of two stocks whose prices are positively and negatively correlated to the price of oil.

FinPortfolio.com not only measures the risk of a portfolio, but also suggests changes to it that optimize the risk/reward profile.

Figure 13-1 details a portfolio that includes Southwest Airlines (LUV) and Exxon Mobile Oil (XOM). It consists of equal principal amounts of each security, assumed to have been purchased at the closing prices of July 25, 2000.

As Figure 13-2 shows, these two securities tend to be negatively correlated because, unlike an oil company, airlines are hurt by an increase in oil prices.

FIGURE 13-2

Chart of Southwest Airlines and Exxon Mobile from MSN

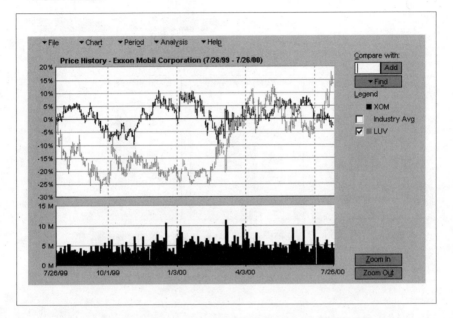

As Figure 13-3 shows, FinPortfolio estimates portfolio return and volatility and compares it to that of the S&P 500. Both Average Return (including price appreciation) and Volatility (of Average Return) are taken from recent history. They represent a forecast only in the sense that, lacking any better opinion, the best estimate for future return is that of the past. However, the best estimate is not necessarily a good estimate. Return is therefore the least trustworthy statistic produced by portfolio management models.

The Sharpe Ratio is a measure of risk-adjusted return that can be used to compare portfolios. In this example, although the return of the test portfolio was slightly higher than that of the

FIGURE 13-3

Risk-Adjusted Return Report from FinPortfolio

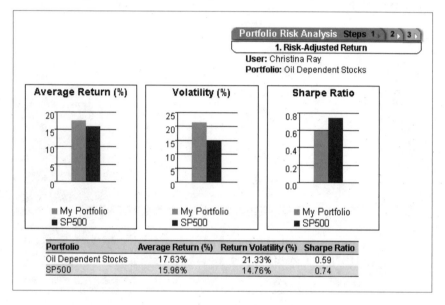

S&P 500, its volatility was much higher, making the portfolio inferior to the S&P 500 on a risk-adjusted basis.

FinPortfolio also estimates *VaR* (Value at Risk) over a one-day and a one-month horizon, and compares it to the S&P 500. VaR is the key number used by most risk managers to express the risk of a portfolio, and is a statistic that measures the expected one-day loss in the worst five percent of market scenarios. It's particularly useful because it's denominated in dollars rather than percentages or ratios.

As Figure 13-4 shows, the daily VaR of the portfolio is $3654, meaning it is 95 percent likely that the portfolio will not lose more than that amount in one day. Likewise, the monthly VaR of the portfolio is $16,745, meaning it is 95 percent likely the portfolio will not lose more than that amount in one month. An investor holding this portfolio must be comfortable with losses at least this large, because they can be expected to occur one in 20 times.

Note that the monthly VaR is only about five times as large as daily VaR, rather than 22 (trading days per month) times as large. This is so because risk increases as the square root of time. For example, the risk over a four-day horizon is twice that of the risk over a one-day horizon.

FIGURE 13-4

Value at Risk Report from FinPortfolio

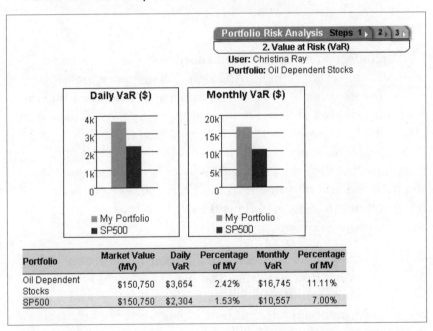

FIGURE 13-5

Market Exposure Report from FinPortfolio

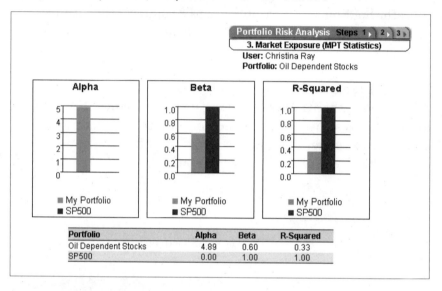

FinPortfolio also measures the exposure of the portfolio to general market movement. As Figure 13-5 shows, *Beta* measures its volatility of returns relative to the S&P 500, and is an oft-reported statistic used in comparing portfolios to each other. *Alpha* represents the extent to which a portfolio's return exceeds or falls short of that of the S&P 500. R squared calculates the degree of correlation between the movement in the portfolio and movement in the S&P 500. For example, R squared of the test portfolio is 0.33, which means its behavior will track the S&P 500 imperfectly.

Finally, FinPortfolio suggests a restructuring of the portfolio to optimize its risk/reward ratio. The user is allowed to define some boundary conditions (for example, minimum and maximum investments in particular stocks or sectors), but in this particular example, asset reallocation was unconstrained.

CHAPTER 13 Portfolio Optimization

As Figure 13–6 shows, an investor can move further up the Efficient Frontier curve by selling some Mobile Exxon and reinvesting the proceeds in Southwest Airlines. By doing so, the investor can expect to receive the maximum return for that level of risk.

FIGURE 13-6

Asset Allocation Report from FinPortfolio

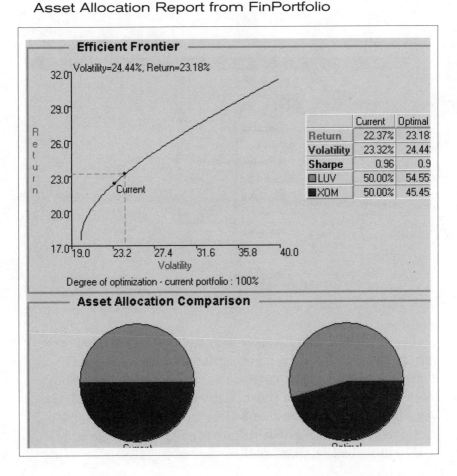

PERFORMING AN ASSET SEARCH

Source: FinPortfolio.com

Price: Free and Premium

FIGURE 13-7

Quantitative Criteria for Portfolio Asset Selection of July 28, 2000, from FinPortfolio

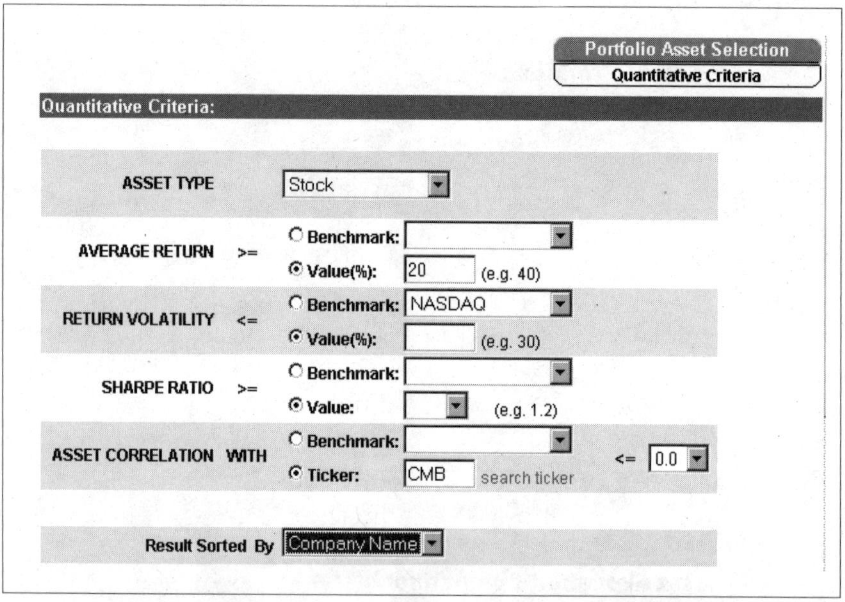

```
Portfolio Asset Selection
                                                     Quantitative Criteria
Quantitative Criteria:

       ASSET TYPE        Stock

                         ○ Benchmark:
   AVERAGE RETURN  >=
                         ● Value(%):    20        (e.g. 40)
                         ○ Benchmark:  NASDAQ
   RETURN VOLATILITY <=
                         ● Value(%):             (e.g. 30)
                         ○ Benchmark:
      SHARPE RATIO  >=
                         ● Value:                 (e.g. 1.2)
                         ○ Benchmark:
 ASSET CORRELATION WITH                                        <=  0.0
                         ● Ticker:     CMB    search ticker

            Result Sorted By  Company Name
```

FinPortfolio allows an investor to search for assets that meet certain return, volatility, and correlation criteria. Figure 13–7 shows the specifications for one search: The asset must be a stock, its average return must be greater than 20 percent, the volatility of that return must be less than that of the Nasdaq index, and its correlation with Chase Manhattan Corporation (CMB) must be less than −0.1 (somewhat negatively correlated).

FIGURE 13-8

Search Result for Asset Selection of July 28, 2000, from FinPortfolio

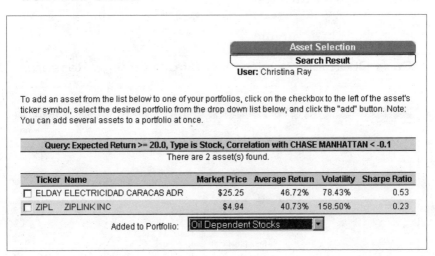

Figure 13–8 shows the results of the search. It identified two securities that met the criteria: Electricidad Caracas (a foreign utility) and Ziplink (an integrated network provider for Internet ISPs). An investor anticipating combining Chase with one of these two securities must first become convinced that there are fundamental reasons why the negative correlation might continue in the future and is not merely a statistical fluke.

Knowing Chase's fundamentals might help aid the analysis. In 1999, Chase's venture capital group made a tremendous profit for the firm from funding start-up companies. So, in 2000, Chase was trading more like the Nasdaq index than like a money-center bank. It may be that the two companies selected can be expected to be inversely correlated to the Nasdaq rather than to Chase.

RECOGNIZING DANGER SIGNS

Sources: Varies with site.

FIGURE 13-9

Price Chart for Wave Systems from Omega Research

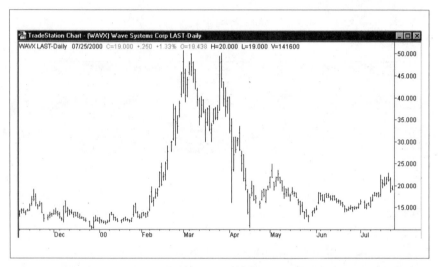

A trader engaged in high-risk behavior can and should use several different sources of information to control the risk. In the case of Wave Systems, several indicators and analyses simultaneously provided advance warning of potentially catastrophic losses.

The first such warning came from charts of price and implied volatility, as shown in Figures 13–9 and 13-10. On March 29 (the date the two brothers received their margin calls), the price chart shows that Wave had just formed a double top: a chart formation indicating serious resistance. Wave had almost

CHAPTER 13 Portfolio Optimization

FIGURE 13-10

Implied Volatility Chart for Wave Systems from Omega Research

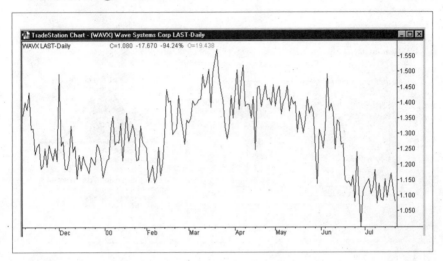

reached its high price of late February, but had failed to make a new high.

Next, the volatility chart shows implied volatility reaching a new high of over 150 percent per year in mid-March. Options traders perceived risk in Wave as higher than ever before. Because implied volatility is derived from options prices, it is forward looking, and represents consensus trader options about future volatility in Wave.

Checking with RiskGrades would also have indicated that the risk of Wave was growing. The chart of Wave's RiskGrade in Figure 13-11 shows two signs of danger. First, Wave's RiskGrade of approximately 750 in late March is about three times that of the average RiskGrade for U.S. markets of 286.

FIGURE 13-11

Chart of Risk Grade for Wave Systems from RiskGrades

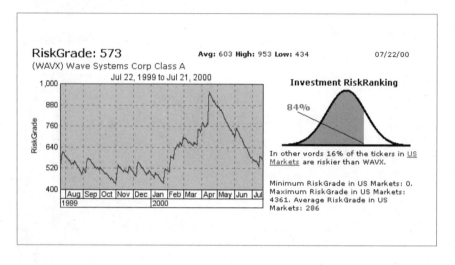

Even on July 21 (the date of the chart) a RiskGrade of 573 put Wave in the top 16 percent of U.S. markets by risk. Further, Wave's RiskGrade was trending upward at a rapid rate: It rose about 50 percent from the start of the year to the end of March.

FinPortfolio would have translated this volatility to more understandable dollar risk. Figure 13-12 shows that Monthly VaR is estimated to be $598,118 for a $1 million portfolio. This means that the probability of a 59.81 percent loss over one month is 5 percent, unacceptably high for an investor without a large cash reserve. Because the brothers purchased the stock on 50 percent margin, a 59 percent loss would have wiped them out.

The brothers aggravated their risk by failing to have an exit strategy. They had failed to specify in advance under what circumstances they should take profits or losses. If they had immediately investigated the reason for the margin call rather than assume it was an error, they might have understood the implications of such a catalyst on the price of Wave. From the chat rooms, they knew that many of the investors in this stock were margined to the hilt and fully invested in one stock. So they might have anticipated that market orders to sell would flood the market when the Wavoids couldn't meet the calls. They lost precious days—and therefore nearly all their money—while trying unsuccessfully to hold on to their positions. They were first in the door when they bought the stock for a dollar, but also last out while the building was burning.

FIGURE 13-12

Value at Risk Analysis for Wave Systems as of July 28, 2000, from FinPortfolio

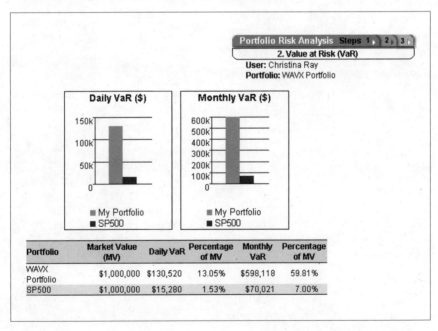

INDEX

Agents, 12–13
Alpha, 218
Analysts, 177–178
  (*See also* Expert opinions)
Analytic indicators, 95–96
Archipelago, 15
Asset managers, 8
Asset searches, 220–221
Assets under Management (AUM), 8
At-the-money option, 39–40, 168
Auctioneer(s):
  computer as, 15–16
  role of, 12
AUM (Assets under Management), 8

Back-testing, 154–155, 161–165
Beta statistics, 193, 218
BigCharts.com, 72–73, 102–104
Bloomberg, Michael, 55
Bloomberg.com, 55–58
  Commodity Movers page of, 68–69
  Fed Watch, 116–118
  real-time economic news on, 119–120
BLS.gov, 112–113
Blue Martini Software, 140
Bollinger Bands, 78–79
Bonuses, traders', 7
Borsellino, Lewis, 189, 190
Bridge.com, 84–86
Briefing.com, 109–110

Broadcom Corp., 72–73
Brokers, 8, 12–13
BSR percent, 60–61
BulldogResearch.com, 182–186

Calls, 75
Catalysts, 121–122
CBOT (Chicago Board of Trade), 1, 13, 17, 91–94, 191
CBOT.com, 32–33, 91–94
Celera Genomics, 153
Channels, 88
Charting, 81–82
  "analytics" as quantified, 95
  patterns, identifying, 72–73
  selection of appropriate period for, 89–90
  simplicity of techniques for, 162
Chase Manhattan Corporation, 220, 221
Cisco Systems Inc., 17–20, 26, 48, 84–86
CME (Chicago Mercantile Exchange), 1, 13, 30–31
CNET.com, 87–88
Color, 43–44
Commodity Movers (Bloomberg.com), 68–69
Commodity Price Index, 108
Composite screens, 10
Conference calls, 187–188
Cubes, 66

229

Damasio, Antonio, 5
DBC.com, 30–31
Dealers, 8–9
    primary, 14
    role of, 13–15
Degrees of freedom, 161–162
Delta criterion, 167–168, 203
Delta neutral, 203
Dimeco Inc., 165
Draw-down, 186

ECNs (electronic communications networks), 15–16, 24–25
Economic Calendar (Yahoo), 109–111
Economic news, 107–108, 119–120
Edgar-Online.com, 131–135
Efficient markets, 4
Electricidad Caracas, 221
Electronic exchange books, 24–25
    3DStockCharts.com, 26–27
    Island.com, 24–25
    Quotezart.com, 28–29
Emotions, 4–5
Employment Situation Summary (BLS), 112–113
EPS (earnings per share), 123–124
Equity options, measuring risk for, 204–205
Event risk, 212
Events, catalysts and, 121–122
Exodus Communications:
    brokerage recommendations, summary of, 179–181
    flow over time for, 50–51
    media sources for information on, 145
    real-time news about, 128–130
    snapshot of opinions about, 182–186

Expectations theory, 56
Expert opinions, 177–178
    and conference calls, 187–188
    qualifying, 182–186
    reviewing, 179–181
    technical commentary, 189–190
Expiration date, 39–40
Exxon Mobile Oil, 214–215, 219

FalconEye.com, 50–54, 173–175
Fast market, 107
FCC, 134
Fear, 4
Fed funds rate, 56
Fed watchers, 116
Federal Reserve:
    Bloomberg Fed Watch, 116–120
    calendar of, 114–115
    Fed funds rate of, 56
    interest rates changed by, 82, 108
    and options on bond futures, 79
    tightening actions of, 58
FederalReserve.gov, 114–115
Finder (analytic tool), 151–155
FinPortfolio.com, 214–221
First Security Corp., 168–172
Five-year traders, 14
Floor brokers, 12–13
Flow, 43–44
    over time, 48–52
    on WindowOnWallStreet.com, 45–47
FOMC (Federal Open Market Committee), 115–118
Fund managers, 7–8
Fundamental screening, 149–150, 156–157

Futures market quotes:
    CBOT.com, 32–33
    DBC.com, 30–31

General Motors, 46–47
"Greeks, the," 167
Gut feelings, 5

Handles, 21
Hedge funds, 8
Historical volatility, 77, 167
Homestake Mining, 196–198, 201
Human behavior, 82

I/B/E/S International Inc., 182
Implied volatility, 76–79, 167
Inefficient market hypothesis, 82
Information:
    and market color/flow, 43–44
    sources of, 1
Instinet, 15
Institutional investors/traders, 3–5, 7–9
Intel, 22–23
Interest messages, institutional, 62–65
Interest rates:
    changes in, 82, 108
    deriving future expectations for, 55–58
Intrinsic value, 39
Inverted yield curve, 56
IPO.com, 136–138
IPOs (Initial Public Offerings):
    evaluating, 136–138
    listening to insider talk on, 139–142

Island, 15
Island.com, 24–25

Jargon, trader, 16–17
Justice Department, 134
JustQuotes.com, 145

Lifted offers, 19–20
Limit orders, 19
    calculation, automating, 53–54
Limited, Inc., 124–125
Liquidity, 18
Long volatility position, 203
LOS.net, 80
Lycos, Inc., 45

Market efficiency, 82
Market orders, 18
Market Radar, 158–160
Market Sleuth report, 51
Markowitz, Harry, 210–211
MCI WorldCom, 132–135
Microsoft, 53–54, 99–101, 204–208
Model(s), 95–96
    Moving Average Crossover, 206–208
    technical training, 161–162
Modern portfolio theory, 210–211
Morgan Stanley Dean Witter, 51–52, 196–198, 201
Morning meetings, 105
MorningStar.com, 158–160
Moving average, 97–98
Moving Average Breakout method, 164–165

Moving Average Crossover model, 206–208
MSN.com, 89–90, 97–98
    earnings calendar on, 123–124
    earnings estimates on, 124–126
    Finder feature of, 151–155
    real-time stock quotes on, 22–23
    Research Wizard feature of, 169–171
    tracking portfolio performance on, 196–199
MultexInvestor.com, 179–181
Musical quotes, 59–61
Mutual funds, 8

Nasdaq, 15, 25
    monitoring flow on, 45–46, 50–51
    most active stocks on, 70–71
    price/volume data for index shares from, 66–67
Nasdaq.com, 70–71
News:
    economic, 107–108, 119–120
    keeping up with, 143–144
    real-time alerts of, 127–130
Nokia, 62–64
Nonfarm payrolls, 110–111
NYSE (New York Stock Exchange), 46–47

Odean, Terrance, 212
Omega Research, 99, 222–223
OmegaResearch.com, 204–205
On-line day traders, 3
Open interest, 39
Optimization, 192, 210
Optionetics.com, 76–79

Optionomics.com, 202–203
Options:
    at-the-money, 39–40, 168
    delta of, 167–168
    on futures, 34–35, 202–203
    quotes on listed stock, 38–41
Order imbalances, identifying, 59–61
Order Optimizer, 53–54

P/E ratios, 154–155
Performance attribution, 210
Philip Morris, 64, 65
Picture, 22
Polycom, 159, 160
Portfolio optimization, 210
Portfolio performance, tracking, 196–199
Portfolio risk, measuring, 200–201, 214–219
Premium, 39
Price(s):
    quality of, 11–12
    strike, 39
Primary dealers, 14
Proprietary traders, 44
ProSuite 2000i, 99
Puts, 75

Quote.com, 38–41, 45–47, 74–75
Quotezart.com, 28–29, 59–61

Research Wizard, 169–171
Risk, 8–9, 191–192
    for equity options, 204–205
    event, 212

INDEX

Risk (*Cont.*):
  as forecast, 195
  measurement of, 193–195,
    214–219
  for options on futures, 202–203
  portfolio, 200–201
Risk Metrics, Inc., 200
RiskGrades.com, 200–201, 223–224
ROI (Return on Investment), 8–9
Rumors, real-time alerts of,
  127–130

Salton, Inc., 89–90, 97–98
Schweitzer, Mayer, 64
Screening:
  fundamental, 149–150, 156–157
  technical, 161–162
  for trade ideas, 151–153
  visual, 173–175
Searches:
  asset, 220–221
  option parameters, based on,
    166–172
Serial correlation, 82
Sharpe Ratio, 215–216
Size, 17–18
Solectron Corp., 144
Sources of information, 1
Southwest Airlines, 214–215, 219
Spiders, 66
Sprint Corp., 38–41, 131–135
Squawk box, 43, 80, 107
Statistical volatility, 167
Statistics, 194
StreetEvents.com, 187–188
Strike prices, 39
Super-interest messages, 63
Support.com Inc., 137–138, 141–142

Tachyon Systems, 51
Technical screening, 161–162
Technical trading, 81
Technical training models, 161–162
Technicians, 73, 82
TheFlyOnTheWall.com, 127–130,
  139–142
ThomsonInvest.net, 62–65
3DStockCharts.com, 26–27, 48–49
Time decay, 39
Time value, 39
Tracker, 173–175
Trade Deficit, 108
Traders:
  five-year, 14
  jargon used by, 16–17
  proprietary, 44
  psychology of, 83
  visual orientation of, 81
TradeSignals.com:
  customizing commodity watch
    screen from, 36–37
  quotes for options on futures on,
    34–35
TradeStation.com, 99–101, 206–208
TradingMarkets.com, 189–190
Trends, 95–96
  identifying changes in, 97–98
  lines, trend, 87–88
Trigger events, 3–4, 83
Trigger levels, identifying, 72–73
Triple witching hour, 41

Undervalued stocks, 150
Unemployment Report, 31
U.S. Clearing, 212
U.S. Treasury bonds, 13–15, 18,
  55–58

Validea.com, 143–144
Value:
    graphic representations of, 158–160
    intrinsic, 39
    time, 39
Value investing, 81
VaR (Value at Risk), 216–217
VIX (COBE Market Volatility Index), 102, 104
Volatility:
    historical, 77, 167
    identifying changes in, 102–104
    implied, 76–79, 167
    statistical, 167

WallStreetCity.com, 156–157, 163–172

Wave Systems Corp., 211–213, 222–225
Weisel, Thomas, 79
Wells Fargo & Company, 171
WindowOnWallStreet.com, 10, 45–47

XLoss, 201

Yahoo!, 24–25, 28, 87–88
Yahoo.com, 109–111
Yield curve, 56
Yupik (Eskimo language), 16

Ziplink, 221

ABOUT THE AUTHOR

Christina Ray is the managing member of Guarnerius Management, LLC, a risk management consulting firm. She has traded financial derivatives since its inception in 1977 and, in that time, has managed trading and research at such prestigious firms as Daiwa Securities America, Drexel Burnham, and A.G. Becker Paribas. Ray also wrote *The Bond Market: Trading and Risk Management*.